KNOWLEDGE IN THE BLOOD

MACDARA WOODS

NEW & SELECTED POEMS

The Dedalus Press
24 The Heath ~ Cypress Downs ~ Dublin 6W
Ireland

Cover Painting by Robert Ballagh

ISBN 1 901233 62 6 (paper)
ISBN 1 901233 63 4 (bound)

Dedalus Press books are represented and distributed in the U.S.A.
and Canada by **Dufour Editions Ltd.**, P.O. Box 7, Chester
Springs, Pennsylvania 19425
in the UK by **Central Books**, 99 Wallis Road, London E9 5LN

The Dedalus Press receives financial assistance from
An Chomhairle Ealaíon, The Arts Council, Ireland.
Printed in Dublin by Colour Books Ltd

FOR NIALL – STILL REMINDING ME

The street sign in Harfleur reads
"Rue Frédéric Chopin – Compositeur
Français" and then the dates: that's it
et comme ils m'ont fait danser la tête
ces mazurkas ces polonaises
factual cattle-cars rattling East
to the edge of the world in the frost

Son – you must tell them I kept
the hearth-stone sweet
and a clean-burning fire in the grate
please tell them
dis que j'étais invisible
— même imaginaire — should they ask:
let them know I was never a fantasist

CONTENTS

For Niall — Still Reminding Me

sixties

seventies / eighties

eighties

nineties

new poems

CAUCHEMAR IS A WHITE HORSE

Wear your hair like a skull cap
burning your brain; lay shoulders bare
like horses to hunger and thirst upon my energy,
for death and disease the offered groin.
One thousand years of horses' hooves
are beating here between twin stars
my eyes: come Cauchemar and ride our nights,
sweat yellow, sweet in the light lifting
from the eyes of Christ crossed in wire
staring in an ivy wind. Come Christ and Cauchemar,
my sweet mares till morning.

AND UNTIL THIS

1.

And until this then so
you sat all in all
beneath a willow tree, cool
where the leaves hung over your hair
and the branches held your face.
And I, had I been there
would have held your face
between my hands, or with
my eyes perhaps.
For yes, had I been there
I would await your smile, your
gesture of approval, and then
as sunlight underneath the willow tree
I would make known my want to you

2.

You see these lilies?
I have plucked them for the altar rails,
Unto the rough white lace once
I went, and leaned my chin upon
The cold of marble. Now I bring
These lilies, green and false as gas.

3.

If you have not seen green and silver lights
On city trees, or morning over buildings
Under demon leaves then I would show you
Sleepless streets at dawn and no fantastic
Dawning this: but dawn, cold dawning
Seen in windows
Hungry
And your face grown cold and grey.

THE DRUNKEN LADIES

There was one drunken lady in Dublin
who ginned to sleep and cried
tell me love if we wake in the morning
but the boat had gone, the passage paid,
somebody slipped on the Dublin line.
There were five drunken ladies in Bayswater
the first was a red man's red-haired daughter
or maybe his wife it was no great matter
when four were drunk then one was sober,
there were three drunken ladies in Fulham
who had gone when he went back to London again,
there were two drunken ladies in Paris but
no time to stop to ask their names
for the train was leaving the station and
there was one drunken lady in Spain.

NOR COULD THE SEA

Nor could the sea have hindered its own two children
walking before and after, though it opened
veil upon veil to the sun of a morning's leaving;
departure, and thus I shall throw no further songs
to the sea's eyes till the sea shall have taught me
the riding of the loose waves: nor will I walk
with love till love shall have taught me need;
nor shall I seek to dress my love in green and red,
and suns shall not drown by my hand.
Instead in these dying days that rivers have clouded
their set souls I shall cut from me what may hold
sunlight or dust so I may live one with the sea grass
and lie with the sea in its coldest shore.

No Birds Took Flight

Believe me now, for in that grey veined dark
I did not understand
Which words were lost, and did not mark
The formal patterns from your hand.

Too real that town and claptrap time
Unmusical but sung;
My words were tossed into a nursery rhyme
Before your ivory dance began.

Each morning cleared the bedroom floor
When only the dead and drunk remained
So gracious a dying that posited more
Or less of death beneath the counterpane.

Forgive me now, for in that leaving so
You loving, dancing there —
(If love were real then love might grow
To a humming-bird in a child's hair)

No birds took flight to flesh or bless
Any whispering word —
Askew in time a hand may jerk and miss
The drifting feathers of a wind-torn bird.

THIRD LONDON NURSERY RHYME

I am working, my love, in Clapham High Street
Spinning my hours to a weekly wage
Weaving my scheme in an English workshop
And singing by times of the nights and days

For this is the limited tumble of choice
If ever you leave the wilderness bed
To run with the hare and tear with the dog's jaw
Function as living, and cheaper than dead.

Still, singing by times of the nights and days
For light must splinter where love will dawn
Despite the backslapping crackle and praise
That gleamed in the years of the poetry bums

When we were too young, and being young believed
That love was the charm for the loveless day
O the quick man leaped and our truth he thieved
And he scattered us out upon every way —

Run out of town for speaking of love
And sharing a bed to support the word,
For that being lovers we still could grieve
And grieving pray want be a misericorde

Our laser of mercy to ice our world
From the decked-out gleeman's ritual graph
Of poetry damned footsteps dutifully hurled
Down the abandoned apache paths.

Now it's time to remember, remember they pay
The cheques and the debts for the dancer must live
But the tambourine dancer will dance away, for
Grey is the colour of the coin they give.

14

CONTROLLED AND INTERMITTENT FALLING

I'm sailing my hoist 15 stories up
watching the truth through a chink in the boards
a piece of dislodged concrete turning slowly
like a lazy killer-fish in water sinking down
the levels of floors — And if you were to ask I'd say
my circles of experience spiral in
like a zoomshot on a staircase —
dizzy to look up and dangerous to look down.
What wind will form me patterns now,
eccentric circles, fragments of stone?
Unless the dancers and the strangers
who refuse to get it straight
the legend on my doorway reads
London: Cul de Sac?
Turning the wheel by opposites they sharpened steel
for a punctured lung on a railway bridge,
an eye gouged out and sepsis from a dirty knife;
the houses shrinking on a razor's acid edge,
arterial roads, two rooms, a telly set;
Thursday noon, pay packets and perhaps a bet,
Guinness and Bitter — the leering Black and Tan —
offense, surprise if you object;
thing is that we were doing our best
to keep a troubled ship together
on bad sea-roads where each port seemed
less likely than another.
A tree in Green Park must make do for a forest
a pool set in mortar make do for an ocean
a street full of windows must make do for sand dunes,
the one action open is captive; is walking
without speaking, without stopping, without turning:
and so, from fifteen stories up
some lives become apparent. A definifion:
controlled and intermittent falling.

FROM CYPHERS ONE TO FIVE

Cypher 2

1.
I can fly, cried the mad castellan,
See, I can fly like a bat.
And at dawn and dusk he made radar sounds
Flapping his clerical cloth.
I can swim like a fish through the bars
Of St. Peter's tiered tiara;
And then in the evening livid with stars
I hang in the College of Cardinals.

2.
See, I can see, said the poet from prison
As he drew his teeth in the cellar.
So saying he considered the sun as a vision
And quietly cried out on angelic disorder.

Cypher 3

Ice, oh let him have ice for this is fire
This place-name elegy within the mind.

First hand he cries out on the highest power,
Taking shelter in the castles of the Rhine.

Disorder me angels, disordered he cries
Pinned on the graph of Jacob and the Twins;

He has a blood red flower behind his eyes
That whispers outwards through his brain.

Cypher 5

It is spring rain here but time remains
Tuned cold. Gothic cloth in the stone
And Elijah the moonlight admiral drowns
In the sliding years for none catch hold.

Spring tide, neap tide; seasons lead on
For this one sailor who saw most clear
As when Elijah, the fabulous charioteer
He drove witch-haired down see-saw roads
Declaiming through eyes of water-glass
His three-card summer time pleasure boats
The cordage learned and the master rigged
To keep his ship-of-line loves afloat.

Deliver him this much Norse lady now
A white chart for return; how might he go and how
Re-engage with his terrible moons of war
For he fears their sharp and riding shapes,
In the pumpkin world their lanthorn teeth
Are spilling his dreams from mouth to mouth,
Who moves forever through an agony of wakes
To beach, a tendril mandrake of the rocks.

It is spring rain, yes, but time remains
And Elijah turned in the stone.

PROLOGUE

London London — it is night-time and white
In this return from fantasy through time;
A boat's span of ocean and an ocean of wit
I've travelled again and left my sense behind
        with
My first green fields and my white-haired girl
In the towns where she rose to me dark and fair;
And I'm paring the light in a private return
Extending the shadows of reason and despair
        here
For winter is perhaps the time for thought
Since I've grown afraid aware of death;
A time to lay some old subversive ghosts
By ritual and bone, walking the night to walk
        off
Demons; witches and physicks now count the cost
Of all who fingered in my lode of treasure
For a charm of trees, and let the dead air loft
Their measure of the springtime forest's measure.
        Meath
I shall answer; my country and town and time,
Green and distant that childhood of trees
When each river could quench my distortion of mind:
Surely such seasons are worth some elegies.

LAVENDER HILL

It's not too many years till they all vanish down
To the cold of the moon from the heat of the sun

Pushing a pram where no children have been
And leaving her tanners in the fruit machines
Sixpenny Annie on Lavender Hill has
More truths to tell than she has time to kill

And Sidney the Gnome comes bicycling down
By the Queen of Castille into Wandsworth town
Where the sad Duke of Cambridge locked in his head
Says Jones shut up shop, take the bookie to bed

But Miss Jones the ailing newsagent maid
Waits for the words which have never been said —
When peace is the conflict, peace by decree
In the peace fallout, slowly — O who will have me,

Sees the quick boys in Clapham — fame is the ton —
And the writ-waving landlords waiting to dun
On the door of the teahouse. The Pakistan Moon,
Are the star of the occident later or soon

It's not too many years till they go underground
As deep as was buried and never was found

Poor Sailor who waits for the call from the grave
Swears to fifty bad years since real ale was brewed
He tightens his life belt and says on the blink
You sups four or five pints and you ain't 'ad a drink

While Muscles in panic on Battersea Bridge
Cries four thirty two there's an hour left to live
The French Lady slides away out on the tide
With ten purple dogs and the devil inside

And Jim Fish the baker admits that he's scared
His hands shake so badly he can't shape the bread
But latched to a standard, traversing the rough,
He laughs tap a new barrel one's never enough

For the man in the moustache awaiting his friend
Who is keeping and holding his shattered left hand
But there's no fear of dying no sound of a song
And we all need an anthem to play out the end

THE DARK SOBRIETEE

In the confines of the public park
and the blooming of sandragon trees
I met a fair haired woman
who said soldier follow me
Ah then no my love I answered
for I know love's company
they would fix me and fact find me
in the dark sobriety

By the confines of the ocean
and the serpentining sea
I met a dark haired woman
who said sailor sail for me
Ah then no my love I answered
there are seven riding seas
and the course is reckoned dead dear
by the dark sobriety

In the confines of the city
and the evening flying free
I met the rarest woman
who said poet follow me
Ah then no my love I answered
I have prayed and drunk the lees
and what's left me now is searching
for the dark sobriety

THE SIXTEENTH KIND OF FEAR

Who was it moving the curtain then?
Only the wind, the hand of the wind.

And who was it making light dance in the wind?
Only the sea-light caressing the sun.

Who was that walking when night came down?
Just a night-watchman thinking of home.

And whose was the face at my mountain window?
Only a dead tree white as a bone.

Whose was the fever then, cold in the sun?
Only my love's when my love lies alone.

And who is the stranger I meet in the evening?
Only the future, love, coming and going.

JUST A PRIVATE PILGRIMAGE

Strategic grey birds rose up from the roots,
flew shale-eyed in sunrise across the rocks
of our Mexican, our coffee-and-brandy-bonded mountain
over Clew Bay and County Mayo.
I mean the pilgrim church looked Mexican
and lost for a drifting Western hero, though
it held its foundation in bog and rock and rain;
in public barefoot suffering between the shrines
and stalls and cups of tea and water urns.

A compliment. I don't know really what I mean,
for we've been blown adrift like leaves on railway platforms
between the rush and vacant spaces of the trains:
Clapham Junction, Clapham North; in Mortlake, Richmond, Cheam,
in opaque London morning time. Red brick, black stone
and sliding streets. Nothing much remembered
but the names: thank God the chart is lost and gone.
But still, I was aware
with some few friends in the public parks
that the countess slept afar —
in dark and light in Leeson Street
bedraggled flowers and tangled hair

Decimal D. Sec. Drinks in a Bar in Marrakesh

Diminishing perspectives but these of sound
mixed like the pigments of his hand
and out of green and swivelled eyes
the white guide leans and shuffles tongues.
A bright bazaar he operates
and nightly glides through shapes.
Some phrases, yes, of English
(Decimal I'm speaking of the ratings)
"you like my yellow slippers or do I introduce" —
the choir of fallen angels in the fallen loft
lift up the paper curtain of the smoke,
nod sometimes sideways and give voice —-
"you like my pretty slippers" and his voices crack
in circles; but never mind, his eyes are bright
while gloved in black his mind climbs up
until in triumph (pause) he then replies
(who asked the questions voices far apart)
— yes red — yes black — and I keep count.
Ah Decimal: five live fowl make up a hand
a bottle of chilled water and a glass of wine
and no you cannot play without the knave
who fumbles words with his sliding mouth —
so guard your cardboard fingers on the page;
the knave in truth though not the ace
is upside down; is curious and high.

Jadis si je me souviens...
thinks Decimal crossing the Djemaa el Fna
"...and sable lady how I thought
that I had found my countess there
a brocade lady in a bar
whose mouth could counterpoise her stare
and split monopolistic chatter."

24

And Decimal! I swear
not one, but many nights he prayed
his friends arrive
Ah qu'ils viennent...
and he might make a statement, undismayed.
"How should I care of time —
wise men make mistakes,
and dead men plague my breath
and some who make a planned campaign
still end up crimson in the groin."

The green and yellow dust that rises from her palm
my countess, broken silver in a shape
still makes though false a very fair alarm
and through her eyelids tells me to escape —
capuchins, capes or sandals,
plainchants, Gregorian interludes perhaps
Gueliz — the church; l'église
without the walls, without words perhaps
and the grand and sunlit suituation
in his quietly stated question —
most courteous..."you've had a glass of wine?"
My lady countess flies out seeking room
and sunlight falls down drowning felled by incense
inflamed by daylight — bullets criss-crossed in the sun
asquint in mid-week afternoon
Decimal moves through the cedar wood
— red wool clacking on the loom —
and arm in arm they stroll among the souks.
"You like my terra cotta city or should I introduce
of black Americans dancing
of red magicians and fruit
of night-time; hiding passports
painting chessboards
of doves and colours and a frail glittering glass of smoke."

And all of this so simply re-echoed
on not more than three grace-notes
is hardly the same as the snakes that glisten
or the tourists that glisten
and wise men, Doctors and Dentists of the Place
the rich people in the French Quarter
all cottoned and neighboured in fractured syntax
or subterranean irrigation
or the sun astray in the chessboard
of queens, bishops and impenetrable thorns
that borders the town.
Decimal, hand on heart would say
"If you have not found the end
in the grey point of the briar or
the edge of blood that plumes upon the mouth
or dries or dies in any such escape
do not read your sophisticated books by sunlight
and: if you must drink beetroot juice as wine
then beware of honey and nuts."

A pause. Then
evening, daylight and the pipes are out
— there is some husbandry among the dead —
the Artistic Angels of the Place hang fire
and the waters of the Atlas are cold as blood.
Decimal, communing with glass histories
glass smiles glass walls glass roofs
says yes, we have a need, but not of evidence or proof
for, reaching in his pocket
I saw the selfsame taking barman give
some of my money for grace of alms
and watched
while the same bar clock slowed down.
Twelve thirty five
and time to move to find the threshold of her eyes

— knock three times and ask for *halwa* —
she'll maybe offer honey too for after all
three painted pictures make a plate —
a grey illumination. Listen:

Item: "Where we come from it rains
sometimes black and sometimes blue
and the opaque crystal of the sky comes down
like the touch of a policeman's arm
and money is often as tight as here and there
one cannot always dine off sunlight."
A pause. Then
evening, daylight, morning now —
so much has vanished overboard, so many
smiles and eyes and figures of the night:
and all such tourist information
barely co-exists
with so much concrete unreality
of histories and politics —
the warlords of the Atlas
and families sent underground
by cause of losing out
by accident of Government
and by the contumely of chance:
El Hadj El Glaoui
Berber partisan — Black Panther
Eagle of the Atlas and
Pasha of Marrakesh.

So: "sable lady see how he needs
as well as storks upon the walls
most sacred and quizzical
or crescent moons and stars
on the waters of the Aguedal

where a Sultan drowned
in a drowned tree's grip,
as much as this see how he needs
the morning sea-light on the lakeshore

where he could make the journey of his eyes
and find Ophelia asleep among the reeds"
sang Decimal sang Decimal sang Decimal

Shará Bab Rob
Marrakesh, January/February, 1969

28

CURRICULUM VITAE COMING UP TO TWENTY-SEVEN

I am a pipefitter's mate and I have my cards to prove it
and I paid my union dues
when I worked on the Bunny Club in London, and possibly
scalded the tails off half the bunnies in London
but, I put the heating in, & I wrote a poem.

I demolished a bank in Golders Green
but I did it like God from above
only I used a fourteen pound hammer and a pick
— I was absolutely legal —
so I didn't get such a good return, but I wrote a poem.

I was a postman in Coventry,
they said it's ten pounds a week for one round a day
and I said, right I'll manage two
and I did and I lasted a week, but
I'm a good postman, & I wrote a poem.

I planted trees in the West for Ireland
cleared twenty acres of bog with my friends —
planted twenty thousand Sitca spruce by hand —
and that was voluntary so I wasn't paid at all
but I'm a forester, & I wrote a poem.

I worked on the building sites in Paris
drove a drill through concrete and the language
but I never acquired a labour permit
so maybe in the end we can't count that
but I worked my passage, & I wrote a poem.

I was a milkman on Putney Common,
the foreman was a ballroom dancer
though he didn't dance much with his bottles of milk,
from five in the morning till four after noon
and then I went home, & wrote a poem.

I was a gipsy in Hereford
picking hops for brewing beer
and worked in the sulphur of the drying kiln
for an extra thirty shillings a week,
slept in a cattle truck, & I wrote a poem.

I admit I was lazy in Marrakesh
I didn't work, no, I just wrote poems
but now I'm nearing twenty seven
I think I'd like a small back payment;
please send me something on account.

CARRILLON APPEAL

Mayhem and murder
say the bells of disorder

It is an affliction
say the bells of addiction

But not without merit
say the bells of true grit

I will own it my own
say the bells of renown

Ten in each hundred
sing the bells of investment

And would you then let me
ask the bells of upset me

Or maybe you'd leave me
say the bells of believe me

Oh leave you I shall not
says the sad bell of found out

DECIMAL'S EARLY MORNING MATINS

He sang upon a roof top
in a crooked afternoon
(dear Eve, and song, dear evening
such shadows saw him hung)
"If I were only half the ghost
of the ghost you thought heard sing
you'd know before you sold me short
Black Shadows take some time."

And Eve unlocked her eyelids;
disbelieving asked him in
across the intervening streets
of the web that held him down
(misshapen though his fingers were
they fastened on the sun)
and she called "think before
you come to me
Black Shadows take some time."

A shuttered neighbour at her window
saw his hand's grip falter where
the cock-crow of a sundial
was triumphant on the air.
And Eve, behind her casement,
calm as snowflakes snapped the line;
and falling is so gentle and
Black Shadows take some time.

MEMORY OF JOAN

Six taxis in rhythm
traversing the city
the lids of the boots
swung up and swayed down
in the first sat the mourners
with a half-pint of whiskey:
she spoke of madonnas
and paid for the wine.

Six taxis in rhythm
not merely her fancy
the gulls were a cortege
on O'Connell St Bridge,
there was no one in crepe
it was action, excitement
strung tight as a drum
by a dead daisy chain.

Six taxis in rhythm
went crawling through Dublin
I took my departure
at the brown water's edge;
six taxis in rhythm
moved down the horizon
like ravens preceding
the final bare stage.

EARLY MORNING MATINS

Although he too is hopeless
and helplessly he operates
the old man plays the bones
(the people wait) and then the
horned and dancing footman leaps
and lights the dark with coins.

Would you believe me if I said
Japan was jade and golden glass?

One cypher still cries by the sea
a silver key between her feet
she cries the boys devoured by sharks
and turns down horror one more notch
the mad emperor's embargo lifts
on the nightingale's mechanical box.

Would I believe you if you said
the running lady bared her breasts?

And then to dream back morning's fleece
whirling around about the room
draw back the whorls of blue for peace
the freedom bird goes flying out
all white shapes shift, their hour is up
and daylight's ridge foreshadows doubt.

I do believe them as they said
anxiety is freedom's price.

34

CARBONERAS

Carboneras
was a candle in the window
of the scaffold before Africa;
Christmas sunlight touched the stones,
mozaics, and white-washed houses.

Carboneras
was wine in the morning,
black suits and early, guilty brandies
— a disregarded gipsy's warning
against expected laughter.

Carboneras
was also fearing red mountains
yet lacing your boots and walking
through fields of no heather
in the dower-house meaning.

Carboneras
was the crack of something breaking
or about to break in the season's ending.
Or perhaps, one day, just a place to remember
as the port of some soul's landing.

DEAR SOULS IN SEPTEMBER

Dear souls; let me say this
"thank you all a lot" and yes I know it is
about time we finally got here but
I'm afraid necessities of time delayed us.
Anyhow we took ourselves
a boat among sea-gulls and sailed in a shut-in bar,
disembarking was awakening, our expedition
among cloisters of walls. And in the morning
when the sun sees fit to circle round once more
we'll find ourselves a white curved road
above and over yonder and sing a song,
or tell a story, do a dance or make a poem.

LASSAILLY

Didi and thanks, look here are
somnambulists, fakirs, mountebanks
conversing in circles (no great harm
by times — more like warmth I
think) somehow a nineteenth century design.
Balzac, flambeaux and trousers of swanskin;
anxious and homeless, some roads lead home.

COUNTESS ONCE AGAIN

Countess once again, take care
lest inadvertently we lie,
for there are times a gracious air
turns inward from a victory

and how is it so many hope
Countess could you tell
(from out your silent silver road
sunlight reflecting like a shell

coloured by sand or rain or sea
or somewhere in a white tree's shade)
do wanting words then not deceive
could the ghost of time be laid,

or if it could then why
in truth, half truth, in what disguise
and why these crystals to explode,
confusion and a horror in our eyes,

Countess please, my questions speak
this time from loving, not from fear
of actions, words, or of a thought. But
Countess have a care.

ROSBEG, JULY 2ND, 1970

The mouth is open, taste awash,
the raw wind howls upon the roof,
scythes the soldiering nettles;
and dark drives boats to fear and sea.
The road bends; two nuns approach me
under a stern St Joseph's stare
(while wire will hymn without benefit of clergy)
and, we smile, then pause for civil greeting:
"a shop?" "yes Sister, down the road"
& I'm treading the eggshell path for a drink.

I find a cadence in this countryside
— washed white flat Japanese light;
the straight haired figures of a yellow print —
and so I'm nearing happy, though I can't decide
whether it be rock, or space, or wind
that filters through the mind.

THE DARK BETWEEN THE DAYS

One

The waterspout rears itself as snakes, and sways,
its last dim shore recedes
in the charcoal four-run tide between the days
for an unstocked journey. No harbour or night-light these
tumescent suns; but the acid bites flesh; light stars
they flash; flash back, and stab in the liquid dark.
The combat sergeant in the mess is armed,
Jim Hawkins in the rigging calls for Israel Hands,
a boy and a girl sleep beneath stairs,
somewhere a private is clutching his groin
and woodsmoke licks through the garden.
And so the memory: dividers protract, enclose,
a faint smell of apples on the cold kitchen floor
(the boy and the girl sleep under the stairs)
and spike the walls and rip the starfish chart.

That kitchen-garden door will never open;
tonight the probing finger finds the heart.

Two
is simply this;
it's about a year since I gave you a poem,
remember: "Balzac, flambeaux, and trousers of swanskin"?
somehow canal water learned to intervene. Panic
and ratchets and wheels on the sombre locks
froze in my mind on my morning walks; not least
the winter image of the dead horse in the park.

somehow Iaachus became a boon companion
in all last summer's trembling days
among the hospital garden's dried up trees

Leeson Street, Stephen's Green, the stretch to Portobello
but you had the long dark summer in nightshade.

the Goddess Rhea cured him of his frenzy
but left me mine as I sat in the college library
Jean de la Wod, John from the Woods you might say,
means Mad John (Mad Sweeney) or a dried-up leaf.
How then could I compose a poem —
      I cannot yet compose myself.

Three
Panthers on the mantelshelf
transfix me with their eyes and so begin
the haul of dark between the days

the innocent blank page that kills

and in this night do I, could I
remember Paris green? Green women from
the underground

an adolescent Proserpine

not boasting now of ships or heavy seas.
a simple chance of dice I throw
on rattan matting in a metro shelter

Encolpius is beaten to his knees

cough the call — "ten drops of blood
nine blue nails in the sexton's door"
such English words I think remembered

the listing street is waterlogged

and the cross-strut of a window frame

plumes like a dancer's fan. Dark between
the days, I feel

such loving drives us on

Four
was that blue light of morning
the grass by the window growing and greening,
the angry black midge and the clag-fly eating
cattle and horses, and the dirt road shimmering;
the bogland was heavy and the morning rising.

And you and I for the daylight waiting
in Old Time's Castle Keep,
for terror heard, the first bird waking
sounding the knell of oblivion or sleep;
the bogland was heavy and the light was rising.

The mountains moved through their arcs to speak
"Little you know of the valley spaces
if our insistence could offer you fear
no tree, no bush, nor aught of shelter
will you find in your restless walking here."

Across the candles our eyes were shifting
in dread of the blue-veined window pane,
each morning demands another confronting
for sooner or later you must face time.
But the land is easy and heavy lying
        expectant in the morning's rising.

Decimal's Liberal Schooling, and After

Human in deed his mentors were
when first our Decimal drew breath
upon the flies that circled on his sight
and he learned to speak in chords;
Strange indeed and dressed in black
(the evening star presages night
and Decimal is frightened of the dark
his birth-card is the ace of spades)
and so, at last, North Africa,
he recognises basilisk, remote, mosaic
in the columned city of Volubilis
Alexander Helios and Cleopatra Silene
most ancient sun and moon as twins smile back
and the dark ace winks up gently from the pack
though touched and greased with finger marks
still such as opened many feasts. A stranger
near the heart and two red kings at the door
crab claws scuttle and clutch and
Decimal runs through the streets in fear
for though in fact he's well informed
he reaches out an empty hand ... and so

Black gentlemen in wings of black, he cries,
now give me something more than dust or chalk.

MATER MISERICORDIAE, ECCLES STREET 1971

October the sixteenth late in the evening
the lungs of the trees ordain;
the crab, the begonia, the tight-avised mollusc,
are points in the landscape's change.

Once it was evening
coloured by vineyards
a bright yellow bottle
deep in my pocket

Calmly we walked through the dead mimosas,
the skeletal flowers insist —
the broken shoes and the rag and taggle clothing
for a journey that should have meant Greece.

Once it was evening
a dark sea was rising
the blood of the wine-skin
freckled my throat

Near the Virgin's Chain we slept on the hillside —
the Gorge of Verdun demands
flesh for its bracken, the first teeth of winter,
the church bells were far distant islands of sound.

Once it was evening
a red bird was screaming
the heat of the cognac
was sun in the mouth

October the sixteenth late in the evening
the rules of the game obtain;
when I moved like a spider weaving my footsteps,
instinctive I carried no blueprint or plan.

And now it is morning
the sea has receded —
cold weight of the shoreline
that crushes me in

RELEASE PAPERS

Late October and I'm out
on a fair day you might say for Dublin
but a cold day for the breeze block Qasbah
down at the bottom of the garden, its
lizard eyes thin slits of light
for the sun to hide in corners.
Kennedy's snug is shaped like a ship
time and the clock collide
forever taking each other to task
and smoke, like a sluggish anaconda,
recoils and glides on polished glass.
A fair day you might say, for a market,
or driving heavy beasts to the buyers
along the first rime-frost of the roadside.
So much for reality: the warm smell of cattle,
thick coats hot whiskies and ash-sticks
prodding the side-stepping bullocks.
So much for late October and the season,
a cruel five month journey into March
and the frozen fields all scorched of shelter
as the clock and the year run down.
La Grande Armée crosses the stubble land
as the teeth of a harrow rake,
black horses cross the window panes,
glacial patterns, Cossacks in the shape
of scald crows scrabble on the make.
Pinioned in winter the question is:
year's becoming or season's end?

A Sea of Rooves & Leaded Gables

A sea of rooves and leaded gables
made me feel easy in Paris
each in its way infamous as Casanova's
and each as much battened down; cone
upon cone in the morning, segmented,
opening on racy lines of washing;
on lives (garlic and gauloises climbing the air shaft
clearly misnomered a courtyard)
and the triangular shapes recede
becoming a morning-fluffed pigeon
or a blue boy whistling his way to decision —
the Lycée and rancour of leather.
The wine was good and the bread still better
though both remained from the night before;
hot coffee, cheese and apples on the parapet,
we hung like a bell in the frame of the building,
imaginary wings averted vertigo
and the curtains swung like a metronome.
In the night we flecked our eyes with sequins
and watched the yellow drops cascade
of Pernod poured in candle-light
and laughed and made love unafraid.
Waxlight wanes to morning; shapes remain
a brown ankle caught like a bird in the coverlet
an arm crooked lazily amain
two tangled bodies: les jeunes gens
en numero dix, Hôtel du Commerce
Rue de la Montagne Ste. Geneviève
and poems on the tiles like stains.
Trigonometry of course has rolled the bones —
would I at such distance know you again?

46

Not in mimosas nor pine-trees nor bamboos
not in the forest of the Ardennes
not on the geranium road to Alicante
not in the cornfield near Boulogne
not in the Berkshire haystacks we slept in
nor Dover Beach nor any ship's pitching —

In one place only perhaps I might find you
among walls and scree on the western seaboard
in the spray half-blinded atop Dun Aengus
if your lips were salt
and your smile were anxious
as under the willow you once smiled approval
for it is not just time, love,
but time, love, and distance that drove in the wedge.

FOR JACK WALSH D. LONDON 1973

No, it does not surprise me that men die
but that they live so long against all odds
and, running their fingers on the table learn
again the splinter points of braille, the bark
of trees grown brown and bent long journeys past;
a name in lacquer on a box
across the years, across the years; all chaff.
Forgive me; I have not forgot your foreign city garden
nor gravel paths, your cypress trees,
the endless exploration of your petrolled weeds;
I know the cells, the bones, the fluid of the brain,
you, drying frayed electrode that tumbles in the ground
and in the earth seeks out the waning moon —
& old friend I'll welcome-in each deep new year
and eat the speed and flash of sap and root,
take home the wound of sunlight from the stone
and pray your present river air and reed be keen;
as mine, your best works stand unfinished...
spring time and autumn, a circle of bright roads

Oh God deny me not the time to learn my own design —
an old man in blue evenings beyond the fear of windows
who answers clearly through the falsity of lines
that life is, is glorious, and flawed. Not polished;
undiminished.

DERRYRIBEEN, WESTPORT, JUNE 16TH 1975

I pray you peace, you household gods
while daylight lasts, and the globed lamp burns.
Today with trowelled hands I picked
mortar from between the bricks;
dust of years on your packed earth floor;
congealed; new smoke from the sunken grate
stormed like Djinns through the wall,
fingered a lapsed corner of the thatch;
your gallery three oleographs, a pope, two saints,
and good enough for Greco's ecstasies.
This cruel toothed trowel proceeds
along the surfaces, the crevets, the edge of stone
interstices; I come upon a hollow place —
a rooted, peasant, catacomb,
and here, I see, you hid your folded hair,
the seasoned clippings of your nails,
pathetic, nameless, but remembered etceteras
all marked collect.
I offer you no hurt & nor do I disturb, distract.
This evening, quiet as sleeping trees,
household gods; I pray you peace.

Sequence for Carrington

1.

Perhaps
it was, initially, a question of torpedoes.
Long and slim-line; but previously washed,
greased, ampersand made good again. Water
might sometimes lick them, all over, no
rationalisation; no touch of words, no sharks
to seven-tooth the vision, all alone; I ask
for Carrington no cures, no songs, but maybe
a *Malagueña* for example — a start
and always, tipped-hat, slow and easy, in mind
of the terrible turning horn
that drives and misses... just an inch of depth;
how much between the trigger and the fingers
and the clutch;
or yet the pool,
those mad, misguided, farmyard hens
that turn their sly becoming backs upon the nest.

2.

Who laid the boot-print at my doorstep?
too large, too deep, for any yet;
& that poor struggling
human child, partly strangled
after birth — who calls and leaves a master card?
the question mark, *my saviour*,
much mysteries within the mind. Remark
upon her scudding quarters, her scuttled walk,
and when she knocks upon your door
may you be ready — anxious — waiting, for

she is clean, she lopes along a cat-walk,
and stand you back for she has claws
retractable — an impulse from the brain;
& Carrington, sit tight,
encircled,
it is not yet the dreadful death
that seems to wait
that seems to lead you
to the shotgun mouth

3.

A chance glance at an autograph
a name for maybe, or the time called-up,
you kept me wideawake for many nights;
tonight an anvil and a preacher
will keep me perfect in my sleep;
enough for that — but I'd be pale
or tender, bring you basins full of seafood,
oh I'd consume, consuming,
the salt flesh of your eyes, the lizard stalks,
& all the while outside of this resuming
the small talk in the garden,
extending cucumbers sliced in a dish:
excitement thin as acid in the rind,
your garden-party afternoons
leave something tart upon the tongue

4.

You know it was not gentle in the garden —
the lilac blooms and fades;

witch-hazel turns and bites; the picture hats
do not persuade;
nor the well-stitched thatch, the afternoons
demanded much — in the plane shade
a name perhaps, too quickly stated
before the eyes could turn away,
and in the end
the bridle on the sight cannot prevent
the single
dangerous, unguarded glance
upon the lilies and the still, green, pond
and the greener evil stillness just beyond;
that quivering damp unease
that nets you, dead, among the smiling faces
that surround
your tangled, loving, afternoons —
the sculpted head that summons from the ivy
with curved stone mouth & hollow eyes
that see you clearly over all the conversation
dancing most courageously your dance
"a green fan broken by the wind"

CASSANDRA SPEAKS ABOUT THE IRISH FAMINE

Give me that sharp knife, the butcher's cutlass
that shall lacerate your womb,
do not endear me when the knives are sharp
do not sleep easy in your homes;
by times the night-winds slip in easy
and occupy your beds
the dead horse and the dead rider
are threatening your gods. What distaff
could you offer in the compound — ha —
would it even matter — a whiff in the nostril —
I speak of blood and of a universe that couldn't listen:
there is blue-stone in the mountains —
in spring rivers gold glitters
think before you make a time of rags and flitters
& hand me that sharp knife, the butcher's cutlass,
better to cut out the sore
than die, begotten, eating reeds in ditches

THE WICKED MESSENGER

They say he used to send her such
dismembered parts of animals
as frogs' legs — flesh split from flesh —
or spawn in a galvanised bucket,
and that nightly she would take them,
owls' limbs, the backs of alligators,
& crustaceans of the breathless world
& the dinosaurs that sing in trees
while he was waiting for a watch-face
in the early early morning light
as blue as blue as ever was:
they say he sent her shellfish
& dead men in a bottle,
a handful of dice thrown down on the carpet,
match-sticks in a fire-place,
spilt stains upon the shining tiles;
they say he sent her
torn packets and brown paper parcels;
carapaces of minotaurs,
mushrooms in a garden
feathered by the wind;
they say he used to send her
such cold gifts
and bits and pieces of his mind

O BAKELITE MIZ MOON

Jump a hundred times
and then get laid
this is no horror movie
but late at night and I'm afraid
I tried to say I couldn't sleep
a bottle to my mouth
but looking backwards over time
there's no sense of drought
and I believed you when you told me
that all green cheques were green —
greenbacks — slap a dollar
this lady has been seen
in Banks with her machine-gun
holding-up her own
I will salute you and respect you
oh bakelite Miz Moon.
A heartbreak on the telephone
sparks off a certain lapse
a gentle lady in her cradle
an age, a meaning and a breast;
we must have met light-years back
by the evil-winded sea
when you displayed your cuff-links
in your bed of porphyry,
and did you amid the daylight
when the hours had crawled away
& they'd locked you in the close wing
— every swan must have her day —
find it written on the ceiling
as a moustache curling outward
a black and nonsense notion —
did you find my lips too turgid

in the sex scenes in the Motel
where we played the hangman's wedding
with Doctors of Divinities
and nurses at your elbow
while we reckoned hours in ounces
and made it down the highway
& I believed you when you told me
that the road had no horizon
as you smiled beneath your vizor
as you checked your magazine
and you got us to tomorrow
my sweet bakelite Miz Moon.

OPHELIA, SING TO ME

There is a cliff beyond my bedroom window,
four floors falling turning over,
there is a door that opens inward
but I have no mirror & so I cannot see
whose face grins over my shoulder...
a revenant and reject from Cervantes,
formed out of glass & so translucent
though if he be the one I think
there is no surface that could take his print
no casting-light from any planet...
But I have listened to the serpent
hissing, waiting in the garden,
keeping nightly vigil
in the vineyard and then again in Dublin,
nor can the serpent move on glass
nor could this serpent cast reflection
I'll make a ghost of him as lets me
& walk the battlements of Elsinore...
(There is a cliff beyond my bedroom window
and the unappeasing dark. Father,
God, forgive us all this thankless task)
Tonight I watch the silver moon through glass
recording still some aspect of this world...
I'll make a ghost of him as lets me
& walk the battlements of Elsinore:
there is no surface that could take his print —
A strawman on an open road
he walks expectantly before me leaving shoes
and folklore traps and dervish leaves,
he waits in some deserted country lane
against the ditch beneath the dripping winter trees:
We'll meet in Sticksville, Deathstyx County,
On the Sticksville Prohibition Train

EIGHT HOURS TO PROVE THE ARTEFACT

Well now Miz Moon
do you remember what you recollected
& you remaining (still American) intact?
let's put our heads together and resume
what we both know to be a lie in fact
our sad relationship: — and yet at that
not all unreal but getting fairly urgent
because at last the news is out Miz Moon
your time is up & you are coming back
and some are ready here and waiting
come in my love the window's open
& each black fish that swims the ocean
may curl upon your own moonlit neck
Friends can't you hear her? Buvons à Zelda
Miz Moon is climbing up the stairs
& life itself is turning dangerous
though Christ alone knows how we've wasted
& spent the night-times riding sleepers
for fear of being the next day's wreck
but let us get this in perspective
word is Miz Moon you're coming back
& we will have a blitzed-out evening
which will not please the Doctors but
our inner organs peeled and then some
Miz Moon you're home and welcome

ROCKPOOLS

1.

The distance of the glass ordains
the angles between stars and eyes
so looking deep into the mirror pool
she saw light years away
the flickering dog-star and the plough
And now it's little she remembers
her tearstained airmail letter to Paris
where fountains take the place of pools
and drunkenly I sang the Mass
and meant it too with someone else
The substance in the glass ordains
the character of chance or change

2.

The pen in my hand encumbers
both instinct and thought
confuses for a moment craft and numbers
and the white page – wilful as wind
remains the landscape of the albatross
mountainous blank unmarked

But gulls riding on an updraft
make flying look easy
past cliff-ledge and spindrift
ocean and sea-spray
innocent of sepia cuttle-fish ink
unaware of the quills in their wings

3.
In the aspen-leaved morning
he walks and thinks of lakes
lakes caught upon the summits of mountains
lakes green with islands
or blue with hard fish – plantings
cold hard and bare are the woods
in the aspen-leaved morning in winter

HOUSERULES

Hoop-la said my working wife
this woman says there were two kinds of amazons
(and she looked at me over her tee ell ess)
the ones who went in for househusbands
and the others... random copulators
who only hit the ground in spots

Measuring-up to my responsibilities
I called to my wife starting out for work
could you take my head into town today please
have my hair cut and my beard trimmed
for this poetry reading on Thursday
(I was dusting my high-heeled Spanish boots)

Gladly: she threw the talking head
in the back of the car with her lecture notes
her handbag fur coat and galley proofs
tricks of trade and mercantile accoutrements
Otrivine stuffed firmly up my nostrils
to stop catarrh and Hacks for my throat

Leaving me headless and in some straits:
considering the ways of well set-up amazons
as I fumbled helplessly around the garden
playing blind man's buff to a dancing clothesline
stubbing my pegs on air and thinking with envy
of my neighbour and his empire of cabbages

THREE FIGURES IN A PUB WITH MUSIC

And since it has to be a pub scene faute de mieux
take one fat man spread upon a bar stool
talking of Billie Holliday's Strange Fruit
                    Garotted by the slit eyes
on his left he launches into relativity
Einstein he says was only his opinion
and don't ever — lifts glass — degenerate opinion
                    The instruments
I admire the most are the trumpet and the voice
I don't Strange Fruit remember if the blacks were free
he lurches through an instantaneous high C

and slit eyes picks up faultless on the melody
O Mein Papa and Eddie Calvert was magnificent

                    His dexterous friend
the donkey-jacket-over-duck-egg-blue despite
initial difficulty in the depth of field
regains some clarity of tone and brain and pitch
                    (why am I so Black & Blue)
while slit eyes does a private quick-step to the jacks
and disappears the props and stools are switched
on absent friends the orchestra lights up the two
                    with martial music
for chat of history and politics and work and sex
and first name heads of state and drink and revolution
and melting dusty ice fills up the cracks

                    the dying notes
of Tipperary Far Away in Spanish Harlem

Days of May 1985

In the village street a stained-glass artist
Is trawling the shops for Brunswick Black
On a morning when my head is taken up with light
And light effects on silver halides

Or in Russells on a bleary Wednesday
Clients push in chafing and shooting their cuffs
Signalling pints but "spirits out first please"
Such are the limits of a year's horizons

This week brought Paul Durcan's postcard
With news of Robert Frost and mention of Mt LaFayette
A catalogue of timber in New Hampshire
And yesterday my wife sailed in from Paris

To find me dressed again in campaign summer gear
Which doesn't differ much in truth from winter's
The addition or the stripping of a layer plus decorations
For my regimental Thursdays in the mad house

Being thus torpedoed I must have my story straight
And in my ley-lines find a bill of credence
Pick up on Leeson Street where I was born —
In the Appian Way my bones of childhood mock me

Yet these May mornings toiling to the Nursery
I sense my father's ghost in the wheeling migrant birds
And soon I can accept the electric invitation
Of my amazing son to the breathless world of cherry flowers

CLOSEUP

He is my neighbour yet
he puzzles me — he is a threat up there
guarding the summer shoulder of the hill
perched upon sticks and busy as an insect
                                first time we met
he choked off my tentative *buon giorno*
(and ever since although his wife replies)
                        gruff and locked
in the narrow gauge of his daily
crab-slide from the doorway to the shade
and the waiting car seat set
by the furnace wall beneath the autumn grapes

he is a *bella figura* man of substance

                        his photograph
will find due place
with the others ranked along the cemetery wall
the Bevagnas and the Rossis not in prayer

but as now in slippers and woolen cap he stares
down the ridges of the valley to the road below
a partisan planning an ambush

or putting order on the seasons
he has marshalled them and marked them out with feast days
crippled he is impervious to accident
                        or weather
it is September now and he is out to check
that Polythene is fastened on the wood piles
stirrup pump in hand he stumps the barricades
he is opaque and undefeated

                              and why
should I know more about him than this bare account
reckoned against such camouflage
the wind picks up and whispers through the graveyard

that is all
soon they will be tying down their houses for the winter
the year is done

green lizards dart fearless in the noonday vines
where light itself is sharp and green

LAZARUS IN FADE STREET, SUMMER 1986

This afternoon in Fade Street in the sun
all these ancient gestures
and all those flickering acid lights
they... *don't touch me any more*
come home from harvesting the years
I have gathered in my tribe and wives
and tied the haggard door

thinks Lazarus in Fade Street in surprise

come home at last to roost
like a retired sea captain
without support or sycophants
I am watching how the operators work
taking a bearing in my own backyard
on the shifting of brick and emphasis
the architecture of the New Ireland
and noticing the architects by name

Oh Alice Glenn
Lady of Astronomical Compassion
Pray for us now and in Leinster House Amen

and I feel I was more cherished underground:

consistent in my generation
spent maybe twenty years entombed
just looking out and listening to the rain
achieving wisdom and no position
a nineteen sixties solipsist —
thus I reserve my own defence —
filling in the cracks in time until
the door swung open and I shook myself awake

rolled off my bed of snakes
and travelled home like a fault to roost
a cherished child of the State
my pockets full of unsigned cheques
faded unpresented dreams
manifests of phantom ships
dry salt I gathered off Cape Horn
dry salt for wounds the curing of:

no need for gothic narrative thinks Lazarus

Ronald Reagan is made a Doctor of Laws
pray for us now in Leinster House

something is happening here

Peter Barry is selective in his strictures
I listened hard but heard
no echoes of outrage when Tripoli was bombed

*and I don't know what it is
do you Mr. Bones?*

And yes — who speaks for me in this
coming up out of the ground
a fading Signorelli figure strayed from Orvieto
making my way home from Waldo's Wood?
I feel threatened in this referendum
by the aggressive razzmatazz of family men
I have a family but I cannot share
the appalling certainty of Padraig Flynn:

who conjures *me* in Fade Street?

Lazarus without an audience
emerging into daylight stumbles in the dust
steadies himself by the Castle Market
consults his chart and makes for home
the high road home from Cesena
veteran of hospital and lock-up
here's where we part company perhaps
finding another way through the waste lots
turning off at the fireworks factory

and singing: *flat road yellow moon*
coming home at night through fields of sunflowers

Stopping the Lights, Ranelagh 1986

1.

Two hands to the bottle of Wincarnis
this timeless gent his cap turned back to front
arranges himself in the delta of downtown Ranelagh
and sits on the public bench first
carefully hitching his trousers at the knee
preserving the delicate break over the instep
advised by Bertie Wooster's Jeeves
he hefts the bottle up and sucking deep
with one eye shut he draws a bead

Secure in his well constructed tree top hide
Lord Greystokes fixes on the jungle
in between the changing of the traffic lights
like drops of blood the amber jewels of his rood
accurately lights a cigarette
The lion — he mouths — *The lion sleeps tonight*
the traffic beacons change
controlled and manageable their peacock march
from green to red and red to green
Ring out wild bells: he settles back

A businesslike nun swims into frame
intervenes in a pale cold car behold
and disengaging gear
reflects a while in Gordon's hardware shop
the glass of her aquarium is hung
with buses plastic basins toasters
electric kettles lengths of timber super-glue
bronze fire-dogs brooms and Bilton dinner sets
here on the veldt

she brings a missionary whisper
the folded mysteries of convent breakfasts
white linen and starched altar cloths
white cattle birds half glimpsed in Africa
lights flash cars slip into gear slide off

And the delta has become my launching pad
my swampland Florida
junkyard of burnt-out rocket systems
where all that thrust falls back to earth
to rust in secret in the Corporation Park
my blue eyed son is friend to man
and guides me through the shadowy tangled paths
where alligators twine and lurk
and I learn to recognise my lunar neighbours
among mysterious constellations

2.

It takes some time to make an epic
or see things for the epic that they are
an eighteenth century balloonist
when Mars was in the Sun set out for Wales from here
trailing sparks ascended through the clouds
and sank to earth near Howth
while dancing masters in the Pleasure Gardens
played musical glasses in the undergrowth
they have used the story to rename a pub
to make a Richard Crosbie of the Chariot

And we too
have come through dangers and we call
to the MC on the console *stop the lights*

here at the wrong end of the telescope
my one concern is holding down the present
Sunday mornings on the Great South Wall are real
and hand in hand with Niall
it is enough
when we are astral travellers and our astral turf
the cut blocks that interlock upon each other
and we are inaccessible and far off dots
on the Half Moon road to the lighthouse
safe from the law alive and well
in the wind on the Great South Wall

WORDS FROM A ONE WAY TICKET

I came abreast of my forty-sixth year Captain
since last I saw you —
nine hours out of Paris on the Napoli Express
six of us at five-twenty-five A M
stretched out in our couchette
on the wings of triplanes
wrapped in disposable fabrics
we are hot cryonics in a honeycomb
lifting up on the occasional elbow
to angle for the dawn —
and missing it at Torino Porto Nuovo
the cormorants bobbed awake at Genova
put on their daytime faces for La Spezia
where I fell down a marble staircase once —
But no stopping this time Captain
we will go beneath the hills past Pisa
in Florence maybe have a cup of coffee
and make my through connection for Teróntola

Always hopeful of the great adventure
I listen to their heartbeats and survey the years
noting how we submerge like submarines
to surface maybe a decade later
when we are travelling down some Autostrada
and the rhythm sets a train of thought in motion
until late in the hazy afternoon
poised and quick on some foreign cross-roads
or striding some railway platform
you meet yourself and learn that you are someone else
that all these years you have been someone else —
a civil servant in Salamanca
with a wife and child and mistress —

who sits too long over drinks in the evening
in some shadowed sandstone square playing dice
But while he survives I am moving into
another kind of bandit country
to learn what happens after forty-five:

The trees were bare when we arrived
it was thundery and cold
the kind of weather you imagine did for Shelley
and we burned the off-cut logs from the mill
but now on this last day of April
I can see clear across the Plain of Umbria
and the clusters of houses dotted on the hill-tops
bear Aristotelian witness
to the sympathy of stone —
no colour here seems out of place
where everything that is has rein to riot —
There is order in the frenzy of the light
all along the slopes beneath this terrace
I see the ranked descent of vines and olives
Figures of Etruscan Geometry:

And Captain — when I consider it
what else could I have done but travel on?
Is that not all there is?
Yet for the moment now I take a pause
naked on this Italian roof
under Monte Subasio to make an act of faith
drinking black tobacco in the sun

Agello 30-4-1987

73

THE EGYPTIAN SINGER

That's all very well I said
to the painted angel on the festoon blind
that's all very well but
there's no love here no sensual heat
or none that I can make out
She threw her head back
clicked her fingers — What?
No love here? Don't be ridiculous —
she paused — on the other hand
it depends on what you want I suppose

There is a man outside my window
lithe as a cat
picking magic mushrooms
walking like a cat on the wet grass
caught up in his concentration
I have been watching him for hours
and for some time I thought he was picking worms
it is all so distant
picking worms or mushrooms
it depends on what you want I suppose

That Egyptian singer in the background
I listened to her when I was drunk
night after night with my hair matted
falling down the stairs
or staggering up to bed
and now I sit here
in a cone of hard white light
while she sings of love and sex and loneliness
it depends on what you want I suppose

AFTER THE SLANE CONCERT — BASTILLE DAY 1987

The dark girl drinking cider in the bar
smiles speaking of her knife
my ears prick at the hint of violence
with thoughts of a dark street in Paris
almost thirty years ago
stoned high and fighting with a one-eyed Arab
above that Metro shelter
the quick flash of violence and sex
and short knives stabbing across the street

He was pissing sideways says the girl
like he wasn't aiming straight
and... and here her voice drops out of sight
her hair mingles with her neighbour's
like curtains falling across the street
I think of Borges' Argentinians
dying in limelight under street lamps
it is all so casual so promiscuous
so soft these lethal beautiful parishioners

And was it really just like this —
an inner city pub where careless Fates
blast on cider and cigarettes
so sure footed and so self-contained
so dangerous
the smile that seems as innocent of violence
as the knife-blade in its hidden place
and one maimed look is all it needs
to make us human
reading in the morning ash for messages of love

SANTA MARIA NOVELLA

This lonely angular man in railway stations
going home by cloud or wherever and travelling collapso
in the polish of Santa Maria Novella
drinking an orange juice and smoking a gauloise
he pauses mid-journey poised and folded at his table
warily by times and almost paternal
he eyes his Gucci-type metal executive briefcase
his sorcerer's link with home and substance
as if he has just been told it contains a time bomb
and his time has ticked its hour up

Nor is he any too sure of these foreign coins
and he lays them out on his palm at intervals
to inspect them and survey them into sense
and all unbeknownst to him his eyebrows creep up
his head twitches to the side and his eyes widen
as he talks to the coins giving them instruction
and his other angular hand unships itself
an admonitory digit wagging up and down
until it anchors in under his chin
and he returns to the station self-service Ristorante
wondering if we have noticed his temporary absence

But we are all at odds here quartered off
set apart behind a bright green rope

I am considering the kilo of garlic in my bag
its oil and its fine rich weight and aroma
and this Florentine heat and I'm wondering
if my fellow passengers on the night train to Paris
will appreciate my addition to their journey
and all unbeknownst to myself

I have lifted the plastic bag to my head inhaling
as if to clear a lifetime of asthma
bursting my lungs with the must of garlic
I am tunnelling beneath the platforms of Florence
fiercely with my eyes shut
crushing wild garlic on the walls of my sett

Among the reflections and marble of Santa Maria Novella
magic samurai are sheathing magic cameras
a waiter slides by on velvet skates
an elderly German hitches up his shorts
the cool service area pauses unexpectantly
— again nothing has happened —
and the catch of the station clock flips over

Seconds Out

After Humpty Dumpty fell apart
they said they would reconstitute him
in the Tat factory
iron out the folds in his carapace
rebuild him with sellotape and cowgum
three square meals a day
and some confrontation therapy

It would be hard they said
a stiff course for an egg
— an egg who suspected he'd be better off
robbing mail trains
or turning tricks on the canal bank —
a stiff course for an egg
but they would make a man of him

As in the end they did
a man of weights and measures
stripping five thousand crocus flowers
to procure an ounce of saffron:
in Cambodia there is no more gamboge yellow
and at the speed of light
sons are older than their space-men fathers

IN THE RANELAGH GARDENS : EASTER SATURDAY 1988

Easter falls early this year
at the end of a mild winter —
tomorrow the sun will dance on the ceiling
at midnight on Thursday by the sea I heard
Summer rustling in the palms

Listen said the voice
for years I have been fighting my way up out of this
climbing out of this black hole
pushing past the bog oak
and this black weight that hugs my rib cage

On a street corner in Rome my brother-in-law
the Guardian of Paradise reflects
Arabian gentleman in camel hair
how can I have grown so old he says
staring into his daughter's camera lens

I thought of him again last night
and looked for design in our ad hoc lives
breathing cool air from the surface of the pond
remembering I must not be in competition
not even with myself

Listen said the voice
for years I have been in the shallows of this lake
a creature of the reeds
hunting under drowned and folded leaves
with the water beetles

ANGELICA SAVED BY RUGGIERO

This girl I recognise her
from the filleting room at the back of Keegan's
dismembering North Sea haddock saithe and spur-dog
now at nine o'clock in the morning
I watch her striding through the dry-ice air
red hair the colour of insides of sea-urchins
herself like an underwater creature
she flits and darts through the morning traffic
wrapped around in her red and white stripes
to the shade and shell of her souk

I caught her in a net and brought her home one night
as befits me a convicted anarchist
who himself keeps a roadside stall in Tripoli
not far from the Azizia barracks
a thousand miles east of the Rue Bab Rob
one month's journey through the territory of ostriches
a two month journey travelling by ostrich
subsisting only on their chalky eggs

I seized her like a myth and brought her home
to this courtyard market and charnel shambles
my carpeted rooms up under the roof
sat her on the floor and to protect her from the night
wrapped her in a kefia from Damascus
gave her a gold-work kaftan and slippers for her feet
filled glasses of mahia from Marrakesh
served mejoun and mint tea on an inlay table
and coffee taken from the heat three times
thick black coffee from Cairo

And up beneath the slippery roof
we skewered fish kebabs and prawns for a feast

clams caught that morning in Essaouria
while we gazed out through the windows at the sky
past Rats' Castle and the old men's home
beyond the Burlington to the mouth of the river
suspended in the silver nitrate moon
and the minarets of the Pigeon House
until I saw her deep-sea eyes cloud up

This happens in mid-sentence
with our fingers on the page we lose our place
delaying we were caught between the tides
while the foreshore lengthened all around
into a dim anonymous suburban pub
with the elements and furniture of sea-wrack
rising up from the floor to claim us
ash-trays and razor-shells a palm-court pianist
and in the corner hung with sea-weed
a supermarket trolley rusting in the sand

The level sands stretched out and that was it
new myths spring up beneath each step we take
always another fact or proposition missed
and just for a moment we almost touched
though she knows nothing of it now in cold December
dancing out of the Ingres painting
and making her way down the morning street
she pauses in mid-stride then looks away
freed from that scenario of chain and rock
Andromeda — this girl — I recognise her

MAN ON THE DOORSTEP
(after the summary killings by the SAS in Gibraltar 1988)

He knocks on my door at night
the howling storm made visible
raves at me like conscience
come out he says come out
come out and see the holes in the road
the holes in the road in the rain
it is all falling down around us
holes full of water for children to fall in
and he is right —
five minutes is all it would take
take five to walk to the bottom of the hill
to see these childrens' graves in the rain

But I can't go out
because I am minding a real live child
I am father to a child
who eats and sleeps and goes to school
flies kites and brings me paintings
and keeps his margins to the edge of the page
or as near as lie can at five and a half
who is not for the moment homeless
and depends on me to keep the night outside

Tá Bran ar scoil
Tá Micí ag gáire Tá Lúlú ag gol

No you can't come out says the man
but you can go to bloody Umbria —
and what are you going to do about this
Fascist descent into Anarchism?
What are the artists of Ireland doing?

Safeguard your reputation

I was here this morning in this very place
in this very place today — and
he digs his heel into the crumbling pavement —
and I said to an Indian doctor
an Indian doctor from the College of Surgeons
how can people live in this
in this city falling apart
seeing this same shit day after day and every day
head shaking like John O Gaunt
this same shit and nothing else
enough said said the doctor —

Do you realise
that in the European Parliament
the whole of Europe is laughing at us?
The Germans are laughing at us
the Italians the French
the Greeks and Spaniards are laughing
laughing into their translation machines
laughing like drains
like the rain falling on Dublin they laugh
and the British shoot us

He moves away into the night —
Safeguard your reputation with Cess-Clean
says the advertisement on national radio

STREET SCENES : THE PERPETUAL LAUNDRETTE

In the café window seat
looming in leather jacket
buckskins and bodywave
he sits up and says
it's the stupidest thing in the world you know
to point a gun at someone —
to point a gun at someone he nods
and not pull the trigger

Beside him enthuses
a wide-eyed breathless girl
oh it is oh it is oh it is
and just like that
they have it all worked out
here by the Perpetual Laundrette

And I am wondering
where I might find clean clothes —
really clean clothes
that smell of mountain flowers
carded and separated fibres
lighter than journeys in sun and snow—
not stiff with age and guilt
and battered train trips
from Dublin to London London to Dublin
coloured by memories of Collis Browne
and weariness
and the killing fields at Crewe

A proud male transient
          he stamps the plastic
spoons and knives into the floor —

Why do you live in a country
where it rains all the time?
And bitch about it?
It seldom drops past seventy in Mexico
and you can live on a dollar a day —
maybe more if you smoke cigarettes

From the corner:
Why do Foreigners come over here?

Beneath the table out of sight
of their companions
she lays her hand upon his thigh
little bird
it rivets me

Outlined against the inside of the window
with Merry Xmas and Christmas trees reversed
she extends a finger
and he moves upon it mouthing like a fish
licks her hand and sucks her cuticle

Gathering my coat about me
I rise to leave
thinking of a summer in Berkshire
of sometimes sleeping rough
and on the morning after
watching a breathless wide-eyed girl
in a field drink Johnnie Walker

The Bella Figura, Ranelagh

Of a sudden in the afternoon
I found him
lurking motionless and purposeful
breath suspended
in the shade in my long front garden
a man from the pub
who is all mankind or was
Is he not my neighbour like the rest
even those who persecute and...

It is not clear what he is at
red faced and caught off guard
he pretends to be staring at the wall
then strikes out accusingly
angrily — By God he says
By God but you've made a great recovery —
Do you know that?
I remember when no one could talk to you

That is enough now —
I shall die of that
Said Ferdia

Little Hound —
In one of these houses another neighbour
an elderly woman
broke her hip last week
and treated the break with Wintergreen
treated the break for days with Wintergreen
In our arms we carried her
from bed to threshold
by the River Swan

on the riverbank we laid her down
in the shelter of chariot wheels

Too well tempered by the ghosts
and vampires who walk up and down my stairs
clothed in memories of MIMS Directory
I am weary of ignorance
and still locked up —
still watching the prison weather cock
weary of ignorance
and tired of visitations

What incarnations in the garden
surprise — resentment
or reverberation of skulls beneath the hearthstone
mislead you to believe
that we are talking
that we have anything to say
that you are talking to me now?

LETTER FROM COLLE CALZOLARO TO LELAND BARDWELL

All this month of August
I have been walking to the top of the hill
between fields of sweet lucerne
looking at the road across the valley
twisting upwards like a swan's neck
through scattered houses and slopes of olive
to the Saint Sebastian in Panicale
and alone on my hillside
in a rocky space between two vineyards
I have been thinking of love and death
taking no shelter from the sun
burning back into the landscape
going back dying back
like the sunflowers on the hills beneath

Writing for the shadow of a wraith
in the first late August mist —
there is a touch of dying in the air tonight
the harvest moon comes up
on the left hand of the house
bears down upon the trees between us and the road
eleven shrouded pines
blood orange for the wolves tonight
and the white road up into the mountain
looks black enough for Spanish horses —
do you remember Cocteau's horses —
an empty place and road like that
a rocky neck of hillside
hard and bare and white with lunar dust

Soon it will be time to travel North again
leaving behind us
the outline of an imprint in cool water

a moving shadow at the bottom of the pool
vestigial boundaries marked
on Land Commission photocopy paper
or the undeveloped image left
when Niall looked into a well one night
at the Festa in a neighbouring town
and his reflection came leaping up the cistern
like a fish-child leaping from the sea
there was a woman at a window with a fan
and the band was playing Fior di Spagna
next year at the sign of St John

This year next year of a mind to stay here
working — separating images
the August thunderstorms
and the August fireworks
the lamps of the combine harvesters
swallowing up the hills at night
and build a capanna on the hillside
dig in under a bamboo roof
leaving the rest of the action to the posse
those mock satires choreographed debates
chat show spontaneity where everything is planned
as the scripted confrontations
of the bo-peep personalities —
their panting breathless indignations

Not that I mind the travelling North
travelling anywhere or travelling back —
those Autumn mornings in Hereford
in the hop-yards in the rain and mud
there was ice in the air
and the vines were not altogether different
the same patina of copper sulphate
but they were taller sharper

something to wrestle with
wrenching them down from the wires
pulling them down by the armful
as they scored us across the mouth and eyes
marked us with pickers' scars
that had us refused in the Tory bars

The problem is clawing out space and time
all summer the house
has been full of children flies and guests
and in that dimension
between what is done and what is finished
little of what we set in motion is completed
voices come between me and the page
I see cosmetic work on bubbled plaster
screens against the mosquitoes
but no damp course as yet in place
and water not made good to drink
and through it I'm writing lines for a wraith
keeping faith with a myth
in a play which has not occurred as yet

Coming up to midnight in a low white room
taut with the sound of strings
I am putting together this note for you
another outlaw like myself
sending back news from the edge of things
and getting as little thanks for it —
why is it always like breaking teeth?
Thinking of how Louis Armstrong said it —
don't fuck with my hustle —
to a bandsman who turned up drunk
what dispensation did they claim
in the Saturday pages of the Irish Times

for cowboy subcontracting — to fuck up
ten years' work in half a dozen hasty lines

And then the warnings on isolation
I have have I not heard talk
been told to be thankful for what I've got
as I am — and still dissatisfied
and all this counsel on losing touch
begins to sound like a lunar joke
to a man on the moon these twenty years
since nineteen sixty-nine at least
and not at all sure how it came about —
black shoes I borrowed from Jack Walsh?
And yet we pass for normal in the streets
no wires or flashing lights
or space-age gear to mark us out —
inhabiting the day and getting on with it

The hanged man's shadow falls across the page
in the Autumn Arcades
the windows of the shops are full
but I find no wares of mine displayed
no poems in the anthologies
not even in the Airport Bookshop
which is hard to credit after twenty-seven years
not good approaching the wind of fifty
beginning to notice the chill upon the vines
and the mist beneath the bedroom window
but for the moment not important
I am still light enough on my feet
still camped outside the gates of Moscow
and damned if I retreat

Not bravado or head down doggedness
still less a stoic up against the wall

just staying open to whatever comes
remaining faithful to a myth
and is this any more fantastical
than Dante writing of Beatrice
or the aged Ronsard in pursuit of love
straining after a Maid-in-Waiting
or running for a bus with the Maid of Erin
just arrived in Dublin from Detroit
or finding mutual absent friends
in Grafton Street with Archie Markham
for a moment putting geography in place
before the city turns inimical again

Keeping faith with destiny perhaps
which is seldom recognisable
there are so many Postes Restantes
so many kinds of faithlessness
staying abreast of the long white road
remaining open to the impetus
hoping to recognise the moment when it happens
in whatever form it comes
the dangerous invitation to the cornfield
or Olean to Buffalo with Thomas Merton
ginseng tea in the back of the car
oxygen tanks in the boot
the driver reciting slow down slow down
and the quiet pause in St Pacificus

Which leaves me here at the end of August
writing these poems for a wraith
stripped to the bone for sun or rain
with all my naked longing on display
and feeling more isolated
stone cold sober more alone than ever —
I could be gone like Robert MacBryde or John

what holds me back but that my heart is taken
broken for love of a summer child —
and this is true — and it has come to this
otherwise it is easy
Qasbah walls going back into the desert
going back dying back and myself
dying back with the roots of the hillside

September 2nd 1989

SHARING HOUSEROOM

At night you can see around the corner
in the mirror in the corridor
depths deeper than the lake
at the end of that tubular perspective
another hallway and a door
upon another landscape
a door with spring-action iron bolts
above the ascendant steps
the trim box-wood
and the elusive carriageway beneath —
So much for the Set:

On call
throughout the afternoon we wait
for mirror-spots to point our marks
and give us room to move —
the director sits behind a curtain
his pockets full of stones
with which to pelt the audience
— if indeed we have an audience —
playing Argentinian dance-music
and the air is sweet
with tobacco smoke and dust

The language will be silent
the language to be used
when finally he calls on us for action
language of an age
when invitations were spontaneous
the widening of the iris
sweat on the lip
quickening of body-heat

erectile hairs
swift familiar acrid scents
and in that invented place of taste and touch
there will be urgencies
and urgency will bring it off

In the meantime the house is ours
more or less —
full of scene-shifters and birds of passage
lighting-men and an undertaker
driving nails in the attic

And in the meantime carefully
alone behind our several doors
like absent friends we rehearse ourselves
plot fantasies
interpret our edgy symptoms
eat — sleep
parcel up sheets for the laundry
listening always for sounds of contact
footsteps in the room above
the creaking riser on the stairs
a cough or sob in the corridor
and waiting always always straining
for that quick catch of breath

DEATH IN VENICE : PANICALE, AUGUST 1989

You opened a gate in a field
for the hanged man to shamble out
after years of fencing —
and I thank you for the summons
will you dress me for the part?
What cover should I wear
to go back to Venice for the day
al fresco on the Lido
in the Strawberry Beds in the open air —
long beige woolen scarf
battered felt hat?
Smart tie and handkerchief
jewellery and scents —
von Aschenbach himself descending
the stairs to meet the Press?

It is important —
some time today in the afternoon
we play the death scene
maybe naked
or maybe you will wear a long Edwardian dress
Victorian elastic-sided boots
and the light of course will be perfect
under your wide-brimmed hat —
thus far it is a fantasy
flesh and blood but still a fantasy —
we are in a cornfield
alone together in the full scirocco
put here by the make-up man
with ice and wine
and water to keep down the dust

It is a fantasy
in a field we have not entered yet
some nameless lot past Chapelizod
I see you standing waving
turning from the waist up
one hand resting on your hip
beckoning and pointing
pointing to a Summer in Provence
with the Iles d'Hyères on the horizon
and we are both nineteen again
working on the vendange
penniless and truly burnt
working our way to the head of the field
and the water and wine and blocks of ice
in the shade in a wooden box

It is later now and tense
in this imaginary garden —
the strawberry vendor has been
with his basket of dead-ripe fruit
there is a cloud along the Lido and the river
children's voices in the cornfield
and women calling them back
Tadziu — the sound hangs in the trees
Tadziu Tadziu — the woman with the pearls —
but we play out the fantasy
streaked with sweat and dust
diving coming up for air
recording each others' imprint
until night
and the light we know will be perfect

THE COUNTRY OF BLOOD-RED FLOWERS

Looking out the window
six hours since I heard the Angelus
and there is no heavenly music
in the air above the house

Waiting for the dancer
to arrive across the fields tonight
with bag and bandages — a black
silk blindfold for my eyes

The window is unbarred
for locked cells may not be opened
where we find ourselves
in the country of blood-red flowers

Red flowers that bloom
at random in the chambers of the brain
along the blood
and lock into the mind and heart

She waits and she is right
little coelacanth — serpent brother
out there in the forest undergrowth
I hear her hesitate

Looking for patterns
she reformulates her steps —
again to the light of our lost rooms
love brings its own contagion

The Mirror Fish

Too much alone
I am uneasy here —
this silver light selects
lights random images

One day in Vezelay
approaching through the fields
my head dizzy
it was hard to breathe
under the weight of the great stone roof
red tumbrils of Côte du Rhône —
at the cut stone foot
of that cascading cliff of stone
a sick bat trapped
at the base of a column
in a shaft of sunlight
crawled nakedly for shade
mouth open
head thrown back
small teeth small rictus lips

Abandon had I known it
in a nearby house
a woman I had lived with
was making love
behind an eighteenth century façade
in an eighteenth century bed
looking down upon the orchard
making love in French

Years after in my turn
after the reunification of Italy

I came to myself in an empty bed
with all that world
that Ancien Regime
gone over to the enemy
to find the bat returned
a wistful outstretched messenger
a hanging crucifix
small trapped childish face
hunched up — stapled by the sun
to the mosquito blind

Hanging drunk
hanging like a tipsy sailor
or a passenger in panic
on a ship going down
hanging in the rigging
head thrown back and to the side
transfixed —
Santa Maria della Vittoria
I knew a woman once in Vezelay
with that same rictus of the lips

The moon is up
and in this solitude and nightmare
nothing is resolved —
moving unseen
I am a tarpon fish
the large mirror of these scales
reflects the ocean
the inner deeps
this sheet of water here beneath the moon —
this is not translucence

TIME AND THE ICE-FISH

This is it now the lighthouse
any further we can not
than the sea-wall's end
like the others we must drop back

This week-end — in a day or less
they are turning the clocks back
and we will hear the cogs mesh
and the minutes begin to tick

Because there is no respite
from the knowledge in the blood
this is a fearful country this
bleak landscape of the ice-fish

MIZ MOON

Just one time more Miz Moon
here by the lakeside waiting for the dark
testing out these inland moorings
milestones and mornings in fading rooms —
do you remember the rooms Moon?
The smell of rooms?

Dust after rain in Marrakesh
sweet smell
cummin and coriander blowing on the wind
cedar and cream and almonds
jus d'amandes
okra rosemary petrol-fumes and kif

Running before the wind Moon
every day down to this
museum of furniture and memories and rooms
all to be vacated before noon
I hook onto phrases pictures scents —
do you remember the Delfin Verde?

Or white mornings up in Azrou
temporary cool in the Rif
and the smell of cool crisp flowers in the Atlas —
our tiled hotel in Ouarzazate
a nestling cruciform scorpion
asleep under the arch of my boot

Patterns of grace notes —
the bat's wing stretched is a dusty leaf
there is no one now beneath the willow
but blue and vacant glaze

102

and on the stairs at night I smile for the camera
this time turned by a ghost

Looking down now like Peter Quint
I see two figures in a boat traverse the lake
laughter after movement
till distance takes them in among the trees
we inhabit rooms of pictures Moon
ceramic pictures: painted plates

•

Who is this Moon you ask
who is Miz Moon?
Like a trumpet blast in Cordoba
Moon in the morning throws the shutters open
with a Chinese finger on your pulse
sensuous Moon is focused

Moon is wild garlic
after forty years of determined self-destruction
of giving the bump and grind to time
she has time now only for the jugular
free of politesse or politics
urgent Moon is infamous

Infamous Moon
making a monstrous lizard of the road
screwed everyone she met until
the alkali desert south of Albacete
cool Moon riding — on a crate
of Carlsberg Special and an ounce of dope

Robbed banks
became a figure on surveillance tape

took a Diploma in History —
affected a Nurse's uniform
to run Crimi's Venereal Clinic in Naples
until Doctor Crimi turned her out for drink

Went to pieces in Tortosa
from the bodyweight of alcohol and Crimi's pills
jumped from a balcony
and holding six broken ribs in place
retracing her shambling steps
drove non-stop from Barcelona to Le Havre

Missed the boat
and sank without trace —
Her progress halted she is all of this
and yet which one is Moon?
I hear party sounds from Sunset Boulevard
and Von Stroheim in the garden breaking ice

•

Fearful of rejection
I am too quick to put the blame on Moon
her indecision and her machinations
those fantastic ill timed assignations
I wonder if she ever could speak straight
until I remember Moon herself is hurt

No better suited for rejection
she has seen too many years in bars
too many afternoons in bed
fighting with hangovers and sleeping sickness
she understands too well
that stump of flesh we carry round

And what have I in turn to bring to Moon
here and now domestic me
that I should take her sometime lover's place
keeping my hot eyes off her daughter
every old man jack of me?
He gave her a child and was good about the house

All day today I walked the house
and the outhouse buildings and the forest path
keeping my side of the tryst
keeping myself for Moon at last
no Moon and the double cross cuts deep
etched in my window by the dawn

And at this point Miz Moon herself
the real Miz Moon
steps from the door to the hall porter's desk
sound of the oud and Oum Khalsoum
signs her name with a curlew feather
oval-eyed innuendo Moon

Now Moon and I in our separate corners
are much like any other couple
I haul the luggage up
she pauses on the stairs to order breakfast
we kick the fading fire awake
and sleep untroubled by fidelities

•

With Moon in the Botanic Gardens
I stepped into a Chinese print
of figures hidden in among the leaves
saffron horsemen on a hill
a woman dancing with a fan

in pools of white behind the evergreens

By the oriental stream in Finglas
Moon rested for a time
beneath a variation of the willow
Moon spoke of Highland flowers
what I missed most up there she said
was the simple sound of birds

There was no birdsong on the crags
when Moon went walking on the Mongol border
athletic Moon on tour
climbed over tor and fell and scar
horned goat-Moon
kneeling at every crescent station

Restless Moon slips under glass
strolls drily through the beds of cacti
spread at her feet like kidney beans
thinks of Arizona and her travels in Peru
lakes and floating islands
and dipping stone-birds on the sea

In the moist air of the hothouse
tropical Moon at last alone
lay down among the roots of bamboos
listened to water dripping from the roof
sloughed off memories and skins
all through the humid afternoon

Moon dined with serpents
satyrs and hyenas coupled in the ferns
supported by a plinth of polished stone
Moon surveys the circus unamazed
disdainfully — a maja Moon

Olympian hand in place Miz Moon reclines

·

Heigh-ho says Moon and what do I want
running away from home like this
taking refuge in the lake —
tangled up in images
turn turn to the wind and the rain
would they leave me be when the job is done?

Creaking down the stairs at night
with a bag of celibate laundry
she feels this is no way to spend a life
turning herself into fantasy
a grown person should be more urgent
more troubled by realities

Understanding the market —
take a course in assertiveness
build mushroom cities and marinas
read and re-read the operators' handbook
and the cost-analysis of friendship
learn to push herself as product

Not turn her head into a voodoo hall
a Grand Guignol burlesque
smoking and going for healthy walks and smoking more
burning forty cigarettes a day
lying awake with pains in the chest
examining herself three times daily

And going outside to spit in private —
dear God says Moon
I have left my two precious lungs in shreds

all over this ornamental garden
I think I shall not be let out —
this white horse goes nowhere

Suddenly swaybacked with desire
Moon closed her eyes and shook her head
borrowed a bag and took time off
booked in for the nearest sea-port town
and slept all night by the Harbour wall
with a heigh-ho the wind and the rain

•

One afternoon in sunlight Moon
lying on a hillside
as she thought safe among the plantings
saplings rising all around her
watched a stain of purple spreading on her arm
what fresh hell is this said Moon

No *mort phthisique* for Moon
despite what might be waiting in the script
she did not intend to start upon a slow decline
or some day sit silently at table
a superannuated Mafiosa
shrouded against the light

Child of her generation
Moon would always be so blonde on blonde
death if it came for her would come
quick on a summer afternoon
when she was all sex and flesh and fruit
crushed ice and music

Time and genes decided else
and the wild rose grew back upon the stock
fire flashed along the hillside
Moon stared at the purple mark
the purple hair that sprouted from her breast
lake and sky flared suddenly and fierce

Sickened by light
Moon hid away in darkened rooms
watching the shadows of cats through windows
she walked the stone-flagged passages at night
noting the smell of age in the sheets
in a world of mirrors and books

Diehard Moon porphyric self-contained
she moved through all the phases of derangement
dressed in purple by appointment
turned the night to day and dreamed
of far-flung campfires and the glint
of red tinged fluorescent teeth

•

It was not an Aztec dream Moon
you put me in a matriarchal frieze
of women moving as planets move
across cold desert nights —
this woman's eyes devour this man
he stares down at himself in bloom

But a shadow has intruded
some tension grafted on the lovers here
hooked in position
allowed no momentary gesture of desire
I hear a rumour of resentment

reptilian politics
I look again at the Mexican colours
and think of Frida Kahlo —
here in the country of Madre de Dios
we learn our remorse from the waist down
if I use Moon she uses me
what else is there but leaning in to it

And leaning in without regret
the rest is a confusion
of maps and schemes and talk of soixante-huit
and whose design is this —
who marked out this frieze?
Is everyone reptilian in the end?

Hush child said Moon that will do you now
you have said your piece move on
we part again with no regrets
although in truth it has been hard enough
hard enough and I am hollowed out
weary as a stone

Today I watched a bird in flight
above the lake fall faultlessly
stall and fall wheel dip for bait
flying back upon the lake to retrace its path
dropping without regret
fly and stall falter fall and touch

fly stall falter fall and touch

TAVERNELLE DI PANICALE

FIGS

I woke in panic in the heat
floating through the middle of the night
over the furnace of the pizzeria
not daring to turn on the light
for fear of bringing the mosquitoes in
or waking my son from sleep —

Christ that I could disentangle
just one dimension before the day comes back
working like that Gaelic bard in the womb of the boat
putting the bones of his poem in place —
Captain I am sleeping here below
below decks in the worm bitten rafters

I am putting memories in place
and calling-in on disused expertise —
the eel-net in the shed calls up but cannot save
energies spilled out on sand —
like the lost music of the Horn Concertos
worthless as a fico secco

Dazed and isolated in the garden —
like this new fig-tree planted yesterday
a touch of acid green not much taller than my son
already fixing in the ritual stones
roots sunk in sand to keep them cool —
the day moves on and I am come adrift

To come to in Tavernelle —
we have made a shift to put our house in order
buying beds and hoisting home a fridge

putting a new hose on the butane cooker
having the water analysed
replacing broken windows

All these are basics and still I am adrift —
imprisoned in the evening shade
marked by time and that Sicilian cut
sometimes I feel the sun has failed me
squeezing out the years like juice
without even the choice of maize or sunflowers

We carry on because there is no choice
stung by times to anger and resentment but
without intercession still making a fist of it —
plastering the cracks with functional stucco
hacking at the same impenetrable thorns
hammering at the same blank pages

SCORPIONS

I built a castello of stones and mud
and great baulks of seasoned timber
with oak doors in the walls
and then I whitewashed the walls on the inside
put a fire-back and pots in the fire-place
a new-forged crane and hooks and chain
and in preparation for the siege ahead
I laid in logs and charcoal
onions and oil and garlic
and sides of bacon hanging from the beams
and then I sat back and waited
this whole peninsula was waiting
and I was European and waiting for the Barbarians

That German tonight in Castiglione del Lago
drunk lifted up a woman's dress
his companion night-jars screeching in the dark
pesca di mare pesca di mare
laughing their way up the cobbled street
pesca di mare — pesche di mare
her curved gold abdomen a peach?
And in Panicale yesterday another
a madman torched himself and teenage son
we heard the ambulance climb screaming up the hill
the Corriere dell' Umbria in hot pursuit
and I thought of WeeGee
WeeGee flashing through the New York night
shadowing death for the Saturday Post
and I was European and waiting for the Barbarians

And in the end like dreams they came
black scorpions came down my walls to join me
finding recognition in the whites of my eyes
soot creatures from before my childhood
from that rain-streaked chimney space
black scorpions came down my white-wash walls
and I know the limits of this farm-house hearth
what people occupied this place
my grandmother's bedroom stretching away
away from the house and the hill and the furze
my dead uncles standing like frozen horses
and the beasts that stamp and knock beneath
and I am European and waiting for the Barbarians

SUNFLOWERS

There was a moment I could have caught there
this afternoon on my steps
loose in the sunlight
seen fit to die here
looking down the hazy road toward Tavernelle
and the insects fluttering their day away
above my dusty sunflowers

There was a moment there I almost caught
when I recognised my father in myself
not the young man in photographs
foot on chair in revolutionary stance
but as I see him now
looking at me from the mirror
as I joke with my son about the motorcycle gobdaws
in the fields nearby
churning the red earth up

As I think we might have joked
reporting on the walkie-talkie
about the number of frogs in the irrigation ditch
since the coming of the water-snake
and gone for walks on the hill above the house
or dived for coins in the public pool
travelling together through the language
hand in hand
had we made it to Le Cigne
as we made it to the Shelly Banks

Age and drink dimmed that for us
still there was a moment there
I almost had us in a frame together
cycling through sunflowers down the Liffey Quays

that time you from the crowd
played stand-in for a missing goalie
in the Phoenix Park
forty years ago —
or dying for Ireland on the stage in Dublin
or checking your football pools in Sandymount
hopefully
on Sundays before the pubs opened
or hunting amethysts above Keem Bay for therapy

I remember this
middle-aged on these Italian steps
and understand the downturn of your mouth
under siege and quizzical
echoed in my own
wondering how in the end we got here

Niall plays in the sunny yard below
I bequeath him summer and these sunflowers

LES CÔTES DU TENNESSEE

The colours you will walk in little son
these countries that are yours were mine
were magical and strange such contradictions
the space bat angel spread its wings
and came down burning from the sun —
are magical and strange and dangerous
and oh the world is full of crooks and heroes
beware the cargo when your ship comes in
the autumn serpent in the stubble field
those patient spiders in our dusty rooms
have registered and taken note
and hold us in their thousand eyes

Forty one years later the tune still plays
through this April afternoon my birthday.
in the skies above the Lost River Ranch
Highway 76 and the Mississippi delta
Les Côtes du Tennessee and *Beausoleil*
the space bat dragon loops and sings
make me an angel that flies from Montgomery
send me a poster of an old rodeo
just give me one thing that I can hold on to
and the world is full of crooks and heroes —
I have been listening since East Liberty
since West Palm Beach and since the dawn

Vrai Citoyen du Monde like Thomas Paine
of all the dawns alone or shared in empty rooms
or standing by a ship's rail watching
this self-same Mississippi sun come up
down East of Wexford and the Tuskar Rock
in flight from time and circumstance — at

thirty thousand feet above pretence we start
to drop for Arkansas and South Missouri
new rooms new names new answers friends
as the space bat angel dragon sings
in a world made right for crooks and heroes
that if defeated we fly down in flames

STATION PLATFORM : SANDYMOUNT

At 48 stoop-shouldered come to rest
and grief I say that's it enough
I quit on grief in action and on all of it
disentangled from the truth
such fantasies need time and life
and too much time and life of late —
I'll quit this city and these burning shapes
of smuts and ashes on the wind
smoking and smouldering those neon lights
the snipers under greasy eaves
birds of prey on the bedroom wall
and love in caves beneath the streets

I will find out where this river goes
before it meets the sea — and to deserve
all proffered friendship and affection
I'll salute old friends lost friends
old afternoons from all of twenty years ago
unfold a half-forgotten yellow map
to walk Boròdino a while unharmed —
the lock gate opens on the Marne canal
and slow green water spills out over
all the afternoon in Moncourt — Niall and I
are walking side by side this dry July
following the international barges

To see what happens what occurs
behind the trees and round the bend — we come
upon my father skimming stones
these ten years dead and skimming stones
my sabbath father on the shore
alone and dark at Sandymount

118

by the railway track and the cold sea-baths
come back a black-eyed exorcist
waiting silent where the river goes
before it meets the sea
before we parted company — Can you recall
alive refashion this his black eyes ask?

Look Dad Look — says Niall this afternoon
in Moncourt and cocks a whiplash arm —
This is how your father skimmed a stone

THE BANKS OF THE DANUBE
(after the Dordán concert in Butler House, Kilkenny, January 1991)

In another City nearly fifty
and that slow air tears my lungs
ageing backlit figure
in the shadows out of focus
some dark night outside
and time stops still — I am
the floating isolated skull
over there in the smoky corner
the faded picture on the poster
fallen down behind the till
still looking out for love

Cold and listening to music
slow air and punctured lungs
plans shelved again and
folded up in Rand McNally
that woman in Chicago
who slept with a loaded gun —
have I somehow outlived them all
the lovers and the drunks
and all my dispossessed
my own poor lost hussars at one
with moonlight and blue music

Music in the air tonight
that slow air tears my lungs
and women comb the killing fields
to find dead lovers news of men
stretched naked in the streets
so cold so white as ice tonight
beneath the Precinct wall

along the levee and the slips
on the river-walks and quays
by this salt fatal river —
this landlocked frozen sea

Trapped until Winter cracks
in the ice outside your door
tomorrow morning I will ask —
St Brigid's Day the first of Spring —
which road to take to catch
my nineteen-forties distant self
walking in unfamiliar snow
the sting of sea foam in my mouth
rock salt in the fields — tonight
this same slow air is yours
this slow air fills the room

BLOOD-RED FLOWERS

I thought it was another country
and I find it is
another country of the blood-red flowers
here in your rainswept house
Semitic characters in chalk
still linger on the gate-post
not washed away by the wind and rain —
through the same distorting lens
of leaded glass I see
mad creatures climb the garden wall

And finding out again again
that no one constitutes a harbour
just another afternoon of rain
and turning round and round
in an inflammatory circle — so
to pick up all the pieces now
whose job is that? To sort
through all this durable detritus
these weary sentences
those unfinished bits of glass

With no names engraved thereon
that's it? I should have given up
on it? Long since? You think?
Kept one eye always on the clock and left
before the neon lights came on
been ready to accept the gifts
of emptiness and avocado stones
and then put on my hat and coat
to follow the French accordeon
out again past the edge of town

Should have done but didn't
not even when the set collapsed
and the rustic roof fell in
in a shower of Tarot cards
with the balcony in bits I was
still the stroller on the boulevard
lost in that El Paso game of dice
looking for a way into your space
with no words left to say
still spinning to the end of play

And yet for us I never doubted
but that we are kindred in the skin
with all the same desires regrets
we can put on take off the secret parts
like gloves — in the park today
three figures called me in the rain
to join them in a shadow game
of moving on to answer
to the whisper on the phone -
I need to make you want to make
you come to me you'll come

INTERIOR : THE GREAT FISH

What fails me then to get to this
so empty — empty as an eggshell in the grass —
but May again triumphalist?
Laburnum lilac chestnut dust
the gutters of the sunlit road
another year has come and gone
and Niall just turned nine
he tells me now is feeling almost ten:
fearful for the human heart
I try to put a gloss on this

And think of Dr Hook and Lucy Jordan
who'll never ride through Paris with
the warm wind in her hair —
this time in Paris last year
half-translated I sat down to make a note
in sunlight in the Rue Berzelius —
no bad thing either
to stop alone at some oasis —
holding a virgin telecarte
still hooked-up to the Universe

It's not enough but it may do
in time to put an edge on things
to find a way back in
without traduction — swamp creatures once
we now come down to water here
between the trees beside this pool
and make display of well-oiled parts:
among the bones and tracks of dinosaurs
we too can leave
the marks of marvellous birds

DISTANCES : SOUTH MISSOURI, NOVEMBER 1991

Glimpsed from a Greyhound Bus
the eighteen-wheeler reads
Grief Brothers on the highway
and we're pitching down
Interstate 44 from St Louis
in the snow — driven
by a Born Again Christian
whose Night Rider eyes contain
the certainty of resurrection
beyond tomorrow and the bill-boards

Tonight I read-off history
reading off the magic names
rocketing past the Meramec Caverns
Six Flags Over Mid-America
Eureka Bourbon Cuba
Sullivan and Lebanon
Waynesville and Fort Leonard Wood
all Legend and the Legend is
Explanation of Symbols
or *How To Determine Distance*

Tomorrow or the next day
you will take me to a hidden place
of upland silences — the road
leads down into the lake
and we move off into the winter hills
to eat persimmons and black walnuts
looking south to Arkansas: in
recognition I salute these places —
say their names: *Manor Kilbride*
Moon City — Hollister
and *Poulaphuca Lacken* Branson

DISTANCE AND FUNERAL : MEATH, DECEMBER 1991

1.

The people here prehistory
who carved these stones
what messages and how to read them

Are only voices in the wind
the sound of rooks and daws
crow-sounds in winter

Are also all my childhood
the darkness and the dripping trees
grow brown and all around

Corroding mortar flakes
pieces slither from the walls
to crumble in the winter grass

2.

I am no longer part of this
but was I ever — did I ever fit
into my memory of how it was

Or is the restless movement all
returning home on spinning wheels
going back for funerals

Becoming part of life
half-way through unfinished stories
and called away before the end

3.

And yet — what messages
must be there in the genes what
blueprints from the distant people

The solar masons who
built permanence along the Boyne
and vanished into wind and rain

As you did too my Famine
ancestor — my travelling man from Cavan
who came here on a load of eels

And stopped and stayed and showed
us other passage graves to read
and other histories to learn

I feel the self-same touch
of hoarseness in my voice — the tell-tale
change of pace along the road

BLUES NOTE FOR JOHN JORDAN
From St James's Hospital, June 1992

Dear John — I miss you greatly
in pain and doped
last night in the William Wilde Ward
after surgery I slept
and dreamt of you
cruising Ireland in an open car
some timeless Summer in the 1950s
surrounded by friends and phantoms
with hampers bottles books
or sitting on a lawn recounting
stories without rancour
before you all moved on to view
the grey stone house in the meadow
lion and shells above the lintel
with no intention there of horror
haemorrage or shadow —
but time enough to think of that
when you come walking home from Santiago

I woke at six and all around
in daylight white as salt-flats
angels and poets were waking up
in hospitals and houses
just like everybody else
kicking aloft their heels and skirts
coming-to alone with others
or losing themselves in sex
discreetly in the suburbs
or shambling solitary
from gaps along the city quays
and open spaces of the Fifteen Acres —
clients of the morning shake

in early bars and railway stations
spin-drift drinkers
sea-pool creatures stranded

Clutching votes for Maastricht
some run aground at Dollymount
and some rise up with flocks of birds
to track across to Booterstown
or settle into Dublin 4
marching across the marshes
like frog-princes to the dogs
some learn like you the code of cloisters
discipline in laid-out books
while others find their own escapes
making vows of abstinence
in meeting-rooms in Aungier Street
and still the whirling city
floats in air
swaying waves of football crowds
come riding up the river Swan
from Shelbourne Road to Harold's Cross
new colonists from Bristol
quick-silver to the plimsol
sailing home on mercury
without the trick of Cocteau's gloves —
and *Orpheus Lives* in Effra Road

The room was bright with light
when I came back
post operative and slightly crazed
my life before my eyes
in shock half-naked lurching
from my bed to walk
St James's corridors alone
premonitory gatherer at fifty

flapping and hopping from crack
to crack — a solitary dancer
picking up my bits of bone
from furnaces and city dumps
split images and sleight of sound
dried streaks of blood
my broken bits of city speech —

In his last hours
the soldier with the bandaged head
heard voices from the street
à bas Guillaume à bas Guillaume
heard gulls and slogans
on the breeze *à bas Guillaume*
and *I'm for Europe*
slogans voices
gulls' voices in the wind
and I'm for Europe too
God knows: we never left it John
wandering here for forty years
as it goes on
in all its European contradictions —
the histories of Sarajevo
corpses at the gates of Moscow
churros at dawn among the dead
a sometime morning entertainment
on the roads around Madrid
the barbarous New Jerusalem
grown up across the water
status quo expedience
and that vindictive smiling
senile Master of The Rolls
Wehrmacht and Bundesbank
poison clouds above Kiev
Charlemagne and Stupor Mundi

the filthy bombing of Iraq
not the placard stuff of slogans
something to write home about
complacently —
remembering our own perspective
the only Post-Colonial
State in Western Europe —
your Western Europe —
remembering Dublin afternoons
upstairs rooms in empty colleges
dead souls dead unincluded souls
and all the dusty shelves
with rows of cardboard boxes
full of human skulls and bones
and human stories — stolen
shameful catalogues
of other plundered peoples

There is a wind of politics
a wind that blows about our walls
not just our European history
Hitler and St Francis of Assisi —
for all that we may walk today
in Harold's Cross among laburnums
from Sceilg Mhichíl to the Albaicín
do penance in Jerusalem
or make the journey from St Jacques
the pilgrim road to Santiago
with silver wings upon our heels
tomorrow in Bohemian Grove
or Berchtesgaden
or some other version of the Bunker
serious heads of state will sit
drinking from a human cup
without reflecting surfaces

Greek Fire or Pepper's Ghost
or the magician's smoky glass —
it will be real no artifice
no mime of tinsel there or heartbreak
but toasts to commerce and to murder
drinking to the dispossessed
whose unforgiving skulls they use
Ai Ai Hieronymo
Ai Ai Alhambra

And still we carry on
while there is sunlight in the corridor
the news ticks in piles up
from all points of the compass —
The winter will be hungry
and the hard winds blow

But none of this is news to you
old hand at hospitals
recidivist of love
highwire traveller at night
European tightrope walker
attender at infirmaries
astonisher and puzzlement
old mentor veterano BETEPAH
in eight years more we're of an age
and never were too far apart
in eight years' time another date
another century at fifty-eight
a new millennium and gravitas
but you are gone and I must ask you this —
did St Theresa give a damn
for your discalcèd Indian?

THE PARADISE SEXY SHOP

Driving from here to the city you will find
the Paradise Sexy Shop
just past the village of Strozzacapponi
not far from the Fairground
pick-up quarter — when the moon is right
lights glitter on the roundabout
and cars slow down pull up take off

Eiléan and Niall have gone to the fair
to celebrate the *Fiera dei Morti* —
tonight or tomorrow we'll be eating
fave dei morti with apples and nuts:
but for now my son is sailing in the *Barca*
Halloween is hanging from the rafters
and the ship flies up and up

In Peredelkino among the leaves
Lev Oshanon eighty — five times married
Soviet balladeer lover and poet
is putting the last fine cut
to his life and work: *A Half A Century
of Love Betrayal Jealousy* —
he dedicates it to his present wife

You should have come here when you drank
he says — and gives us Volga carp and vodka
apple-juice fire and welcome — two musicians
play the words: *when I think of all
the women who have loved me
in that poisoned day
then I remember the woman I betrayed*

There is a filament that runs through this
the central nervous system of a fish —
I do not see the patterns in the fire
I see the fire itself and that's enough:
for we are human and we could be doing worse
than driving half across the world to find
the Paradise Sexy Shop

NIGHT SOUNDS

This is what I do these marks upon a page
is what I do and all I do
and I am caught here fighting with it — fighting
with myself with interruptions and with silence
finding messages and wondering what's the use:
a wind that howls about the house
could bring me home
the stream that breaks its banks at night

Can bring me nowhere: the hunger that I need
escapes into the rotting leaves
beneath the walnut tree: spurious warmth of ash:
again I fear I have lost touch with language —
can answer only now to touch itself
and half-remembered images and music: did I not
go deep enough into that same morass
to bring back music? Bring you back?

Went back among the dead to tell it:
and found my father threatened by Hibiscus
drenched with whiskey howling in his sleep:
nightly wrestling with the moon — the moon
of Jacob's Ladder or the truth below:
downstairs the dreadful sisters taking root —
night visitors with barbers' knives
rehearsing their persuasions for the wake —

Landscape and history: unhappiness does not
come into it — that's how it was
at best refusing to renegue on faith —
observing some appointed trust: at worst

not ripping tongues from rusty bells
living in the fire and not the flame
drinking slanted sunlight from the well
not falling to the bottom of the lake —

Tonight the distant lights are quiet:
moon and time have run aground — my household
here in sleep has worn away the circuits
thrown damp grass and salt upon the fire
and still it moves: just outside this house
my far out furthest planet from the Sun
new-born new-launched Galileos
drift unseen past the shutters of my room

A MAP OF VALENTINE 1993

Yesterday on St Valentine's Day
all the birds of the townlands
chaffing in the trees
talking and choosing the season's mate
was also the Feast of the Cats
biding their time to speak
and seen from this end of the valley
improbable between the olives
Panicale loops like a Bristol Bridge
suspending its fret-saw stretch of sky
above the lake's reflected light
Città della Pieve to my left
in the mist – where the Sacristan
waits for unwary women –
adjacent Missiano sinks into the fields
astray behind me Tavernelle
and on my right skirts lifted
Colle Calzolaro bares its backside
to St Valentine's sun and me
to the steamy new ploughed panorama
and the far-flung stretching farms
And God in His Heaven but it's good to be
even a part in the sum of this
in this valley that spins about
in the temporary Winter heat
stung by the midday breeze that blows
from the furthest hills and snow –
curving purple shifting hills
whose folds of shadow emphasise
the sex and bush of far-off pines –
                    and it's good
to be walking across St Valentine's map
heavy with light and Spring and blood

FIRE AND SNOW AND CARNEVALE

In winter fire is beautiful
beautiful like music
it lights the cave —
outside the people going home
drive slowly up the road — the strains
of phone-in Verdi on the radio
three hours back a fall of snow
sprinkled the furthest hill
where clouds have hung all winter

The day gets dark uneasy
dark and darker still
and you little son come home
riding the tail of the wind
in triumph — tall and almost ten
with confetti in your hair
home successful from the carnevale
with your two black swords
and your gold-handled knife

I feel the chill and hear
the absent sound of snow
when you come in —
white fantastic scorpions spit
in the fiery centre of the grate
plague pictures cauterised —
In winter fire is beautiful
and generous as music — may you
always come this safely home
in fire and snow and carnevale

138

THE GOURMANDS OF EUROPE

Sometimes this year I see
the greed of Empire
here in the house and Burke and Hare
at large in the kitchen –
Arch Duke Rudolfo him
turned into a plant
turned green beyond osmosis

Turned into vegetable
fruit and cereal
those are grapes that were his eyes
red-faced from ingesting
he bobs among tomatoes
his forehead polished
to the texture of apples

Apricots corn and wheat
form the substance of his cheek
his ear a handsome mushroom
supports a bursting fig –
his jewellery passion-fruit
plums and raisins
hazel-nuts and nectarines

The Adam's apple is a pear
his furnace mouth
a full-fleshed chestnut
jumping from its spiky rind
brings air and pasta
to the bubbling lungs
of truffle oil and aubergines

He talks of food
throughout Affairs of State –
the rebel pepperoncino
sly mango wily marrow-flower
yams pulses peas courgettes –
all he has swallowed up
all he still hopes to eat

And God do I not sometimes long
to hear of something else?
To hear some news
of snipe or curlew
corn-crake cuckoo bittern thrush
or even maybe once to hear
of birds that sing in Berkeley Square

Irish Seed-Potatoes

1.

They won't grow there my neighbour said
in April — no foreign thing
will ever grow in the soil of Umbria

The Roman tried and we told him —
besides it is too early hereabouts
to think of planting seed-potatoes

And furthermore the moon is growing:
no seed will take
that is not planted in the shrinking moon

2.

At the start of May I pause a moment
in the cool after thunder
to admire their sharp-green stalks

Flourishing beside the vines — I am
thinking of Ireland and trying to return
to a message for my father

Begun when we came face to face
in the Achill house of Heinrich Böll
twelve months ago last March

Begun and lost in moving on from there —
to Dublin Moscow here
carrying these pages round

Repeating conversation with the past —
trying to keep perception bright
like putting sea-light under glass

3.

Until today I find myself at last
beside the corner of the tillage
reading Thomas Kinsella's anthology

Comforted by these few stalks
and recognising differences — somehow always
exiled stranger to my own

As if I had not served my time
sheltering in the clefts of rocks
on sodden hills where no sun shines

Coughing in foggy mail-boat mornings
labouring on foreign sites
and flying home at every chance

Enough to be here now and trying to write
a message for my wandering father
in whatever language fits —

Fits this and fits the journeying itself:
the starving freight of coffin-ships
and the wasting death of Goll Mac Morna

ABOVE PESARO : JUNE 1993

1.

Nothing cleans the ground
said the Padrone of the Villa Ernestina
that evening above Pesaro — nothing cleans
the ground but planting *erba medica:*
and nothing clears the mind say I
but moving on: putting the wheels
in gear and moving on

And coming down at last
in sun and thunder from the Appenines
with our share of chest-pains
and the engine full of air
that's how we came to be here
oil blowing-out the dipstick
leaving a trail of thinning tar
that petered out in heat in Novilara
and that's how we come to be here
in the functional shade at noon
beneath the mediaeval tower
built by this man's father's father
to give a prospect of the sea —
Stranger than the Cyclops eye
of Military Intelligence
in Crossmaglen
Improbable as San Gimigniano

And.what did we ever claim to be
in all our caravanserai
run so ragged on our journeys
climbing up to all these hill-towns
but *seme di pioppi* — poplar seeds

that drift across the valleys
bell-sounds on the necks of horses
on treeless plains above the timber line —
people of the high fields
travellers of the wandering rocks
with tongs and cauldron?
Who did we ever claim to be
but the stories we carry with us —
half of the cake with my blessing
or the whole of the cake with my curse

And happening here by chance at last
without the benefit of clock or compass
was nothing more
than falling into Prospero's garden
familiar recognised surprises
like hearing the whistle blow
on the far off cars of the night-train
for real for the first time
when I woke for a moment
turning in sleep in Milford
Michigan — or here today
among pines and palms and wild asparagus
watching the ships below
tacking along the wind to Venice
remembering the letters of Aretino
where murder and money and dust are real
as chance encounters in the street
or revisiting the Magic Mountain
climbing up again through
shaky mornings in the Rif
or standing in a wind-scrubbed square
in shock at evening in Urbino
dazed by the light beneath the walls
of the Dukes of Monte Feltro

and hoping to go home again
to settle into stone-flagged kitchens
to be welcomed into conversation
in houses that are gone —
     To be going home like Marco Polo
To be going home like Carolan

2.

Memory is a heavy coat
worn sometimes back to front
against the rain: I see
my mother's father on an open road
dead before I was born

Walking a hundred years ago
and wonder if I've dressed him right
in hard-hat frieze-coat
waist-coat watch and chain
walking homeward from the town

Against the wind and rain-
washed countryside of Land Disputes
eviction emigration — the world outside
the walled-in trees and deep
solidified demesnes of Meath

He stayed when others left
for Melbourne Perth and San Francisco
leaving me a place unoccupied
a track worn down across the fields
a photograph I shelter from the light

Some little roads with weary ghosts
a well that might run dry
broken china in the garden
a settle-bed that's long since empty
all the ticking turned to dust —

Memories of childhood —
pink roses on the kitchen delph
and that's how frail we are
too quick to anger — so defenceless
in our seasons and so easy to break up

3.

Even without the nightingales
these women in the summer garden
of Augusta's house
Augusta Giorgia Mariamne
make up the persons of a Tragic play
while in the wings
a tableau from a photograph
five others dressed in crinolines
provide a chorus tint of sepia
gathered timeless at the gate
waiting for the messenger —
the dogs are sleeping in the shade
each symbol in its place
and every boy of ten
in leather sandals
could be Orestes or Telemachus

There are no mirrors here
except the hazy random sea
no lake of metal open to the sky

breaks up the pattern of the hills
and clouds and mountains to the south —
Fulvio — ten — is Giorgia's son
incumbent of the cryptic paths
those half-reclaimed and those
whose marble stones sink further down
into the earth — the Queen
his mother dark and Greek
a traveller from a curving vase
whipped from the House of Atreus
and brought here from Cattolica —
a movement of matt wax at night
and dressed in black
she glides among the trees and tables

Once more the King is missing
from the picture — gone to Thebes
Protector of The Buttock-Fields
on one of the beaches far below
his waking hours are passed
in the muster stretch and catch of thongs
about the legs and crotch —
here the humming garden sings
throughout the afternoon
and every boy of ten
becomes in turn Ajax or Achilles —
another sighting of the Fleece
beyond the Adriatic
some further news of Thrace
a severed head falls from a tree
wrapped up in leaves and dill
a figure hanging from a butcher's hook
and another piece of shrapnel
comes bursting from the lamp

4.

The mythologies that families weave
to hold themselves together —
Your house has burned down
and *You've* no home to go to
my one-legged uncle's nautical academy
shelled by mistake by the Helga

Crossed legends
of the great cook and the heroic drinker
or the alcoholic painter
whose fingers never shook —
I had a message here today
a slogan on a cup — it read:
the geography of yearning

Lily Dunne in her apron strings in Dublin
walking around the snug
on wires like a crab in the sun

oh the nerves missus
the nerves oh the nerves missus
the nerves the nerves the nerves

And did the drowned man
have his arms across his chest in resignation
or was he fighting still for air?

And what of me — sitting here
in this conservatory
waiting for the wind to hit
the hanging chimes again
and reading over-and-over the legend
of Blood Fish and Bone

5.

This was the summer of the year I hoped
to open out the rann
to reach the place beyond mythologies

To see the monsters all unmasked
moving further into age
where one can make admissions without guilt

The summer of the year I built
my four-square shelter in among the trees
beneath some oaks upon a terraced hill

The year I tied back thorns
and cut away the undergrowth
to make a gap for sunlight to come through

And this was my retreat — five upright
posts of heavy chestnut
the roof was reed-canes from the lake

Laid on rafters from a ruined house —
for furniture a table chair
and hammock for the evening sun

And like an aging Satyr gone to seed
among the trees
half visible against the light on leaves

I came to be acquainted with the wood
crab-apples falling on my roof
small creatures dropping from the oaks

The daily flight-path of the clouds
drifting over from the lake
and all the noise and uproar

Along the forest floor — the slow
smooth rustle of a snake
sliding up against the bank

Quick crash of lizards
through the brittle crust — the
sudden cries of goats alarms of birds

Flying ants and stinging flies
and children's voices on the breeze
came with the drifting poplar seeds

This was the summer of the year
that Niall learned Italian
and learned to beat the video games

In Carlo's pizzeria —
took up karate fell in love
and all the other rites of passage

Appropriate at ten — the year
the post-colonialists arrived
to turn us into Tunbridge Wells

And this was our retreat —
forced out and on the road again
in flight we gave up argument

Seeing who the monsters were —
in argument we can persuade ourselves
that we are surer than we are

6.

What a way to present yourself
said the Doctor
when I got the clapped-out
twenty hundredweight van to Dublin
against the odds —
what a way to present yourself
he repeated
looking down from the fourth
floor of his script
lifting his shoulders and lighting
a Freudian cheroot

Did he think I'd been rehearsing
all the road up from the South?

But that fish this morning
on the lake
breaking the under-surface of the mist —
does a fish present itself
when it leaps?
That dead bird
beneath the Church at Aghabog —
or that long-shadowed walker
that struts beneath my window?

And am I not always listening
over the noise of the engine
for other voices —
other invitations home?
Are you lost are you lost — and
how should I know till I get there?

Did you meet anyone on the road?
I did
And did they ask you anything?
Yes they did
And what did you tell them?
Nothing! Nothing! I told them nothing!
Told them nothing? Good!

7.

What was going on there when the light
became so bad I couldn't see
what we were eating? I was preoccupied

About how carelessly those people came
from Iron Bridge or Tunbridge Wells
and thinking of Ó Bruadair

Is mairg nach fuil 'na dhubhthuata,
cé holc duine 'na thuata,
ionnás go mbeinn mágcuarda

Idir na daoinibh duarca: Into
the second week of June — I wrote —
and all the bright days pass

But not with any record of their going —
our sceptred islanders are back
in occupation — landed wearing GB plates

With Marks and Spencer bags
a weekly pre-paid order for The Telegraph
and sacks of charcoal *Packed In England*

Our super-market pilgrims
have turned us into playtime once again
and little since is actual — they

Spend a half hour at the flower-bed
every morning — an outing to the shops
at ten o'clock

Then home preparing lunch
with glass in hand — and when we eat
before we do the clearing up

The making of the next meal has begun
until one day of incidental sun
becomes another and now May itself is gone

A haze of Sunday Supplement observance —
outdoor cooking tasting wine
amusement at the quaintness of the neighbours

Unable to speak normally to children
but lavishing affection on the cat —
and yet you say they're decent people

For all the drinking and the greed
they don't give in to sweat or indolence
are not consumed by alcohol or guilt

Just killing time with tedium
and pouring good days after bad — eating
sleeping filling empty bottles up

And looking sad-eyed at the world
till all our waking hours begin
to seem like sleeping with the enemy

And here the enemy is weariness —
The weariness I always felt
each time I passed through Crewe going South

That undirected rage and puzzlement —
there's some agenda here
I cannot get a grip of — some settled arrogance

That keeps them safely from the edge —
among the blood-red flowers I note
the icons of our histories

Colonial and colonised:
the stuff of pomp and circumstance
angels of an iron age

Plantation symbiosis

8.

Today the day after rain
in recollection
I am listening
to the new-washed sounds of birds
trying out the air again
and thinking — this misdirected anger
ill-becomes me

Given sanctuary we all should be
as generous as birds —
like deer upon the avenue at night

lift up the rann
rise up the air and open it out

But this is not a fairy-tale
and did you know that I had met
a witch here once —
a vampire child with a machine gun
who blew everyone away?
Who set out to show me
we own nothing
least of all time and space

But what else have we got —
what have we got if not
space and history
and the stories we carry with us

I have a store of baggage too
rise up the air and open it out

Did I not tell you that I met
a witch here once?
A white-haired woman
in a long black coat
nodding and dancing among the trees —
who set out to show me
we own nothing
least of all time or space

not time or space
or nakedness
not even owning the air we breathe
owning nothing

Having no control over others
not smiles or whispers
or night-time quickness of breath
not even an instant shared

we own nothing
       neither ourselves
       nor touch
nor the momentary sounds of birds

and that was the bleakest of times
rise up the air and open it out

And in this day — is this the day
some Sunday maybe
is this the day it starts?
So hard to tell where histories begin —
when some cell thinks
to go askew within the blood —

Or that figure
nodding and dancing on the hill up there
among the trees?
       Or only a wayward bush?

9.

So what kind of dualist are *you*? Barnet
agus Beecher Hedges *agus* Stowe
were somehow there at the start of it —

I remember the winter of 'forty-seven
rattling home from school on the tram
getting off at Holles Street

And peeing in the snow in Merrion Square
being five and sick and seeing
gigantic firelit aunts around my bed

Later when I was seven and well
I ran down a hill to my grandmother's house
through flying heavy country snow

The hunched green bus to Granard brought me
past humps of turf in the Phoenix Park —
turf we set to dry in the oven —

Staggering on through Dunboyne and Trim
past Walker's Georgian house and lands
and Parr's and Alley's and the Hill of Ward

Into Athboy and the dung-soiled street
to drop me down at Nugent's corner —
and I walked out of town on the empty road

Past the graveyard and up the hill
through hills themselves beyond horizons
to the hens that clucked in the yard

To my grandmother's fire and glass of port
and salty bacon on a chimney-hook —
to the fire where she aired her shrouds

And the daily prayers she offered up
for the canonization of Oliver Plunkett
and three days' warning of death —

And whatever else might chance to pass
in our weather-soaked world — where ghosts walked
along the roads at night

Cries of vixens echoed in the dark
with news of neighbours' loss
or accidents that happened in Australia

While round and round and round in Dublin
thirty children in a circle
sang and marched about the room

York Road Dun Laoghaire 1947
and an autocratic hand beat time on a piano
How many kinds of wild-flowers grow

In an English Country Garden
I'll tell you some of the names that I know
and the rest will surely pardon — my

Fellow victims of paralysis and Empire
Kingstown Grammar they called the school
at the end of the Free-State tram

That brought us daily to Dun Laoghaire
and I read the Bible and Death of Nelson
with Armstrong Ireland Goodman Devlin

Goodbody Draper Gentleman Long
and my mother worked to teach us Gaelic
Republican and pluralist

Cumann na mBan with the same beliefs
that sixty troubled years ago
cost her a teaching post in Dundalk —

Today in Monaghan and looking down
from this Big House upon the lake and garden
gauging the familiar rain

The turning of the season and the leaves
with my own fifty years between
it seems appropriate and almost unimportant

Except that all the women I have known
were singular — my mother and her mother
and all the women who have worked these hills

Were singular and real:
I think of the *vicina* in the white house
across the road in Umbria

The way she walks on broken ground —
through geese and clamps and binder-twine
as self-contained about her business

As sure of hammer sickle scythe

10.

We have been
living with strangers
idir na daoinibh duarca
our partners in this house who said —
The Irish? I mean even so and if
we gave the Irish their freedom now
they wouldn't know what
to do with it... would they?
Would they? They wouldn't
know what to do with it...

O Heart of Mockery
does nothing ever change
and how often do we have to see
this same boorish scene repeated
this manic arrogance?
Hard-money heroes coming-on
like Superman in Moscow

and Audie Murphy always
striding through Saigon —

And we continue trying to avoid
some half-cocked confrontation
with the grievance that is history
polite and liberal and angry —
but the truth is

I was almost driven mad by rage
anger at brutality in uniform
and out of it
at shootings at Loughgall
bombings in Warrington
at murder in the streets
angry for the dispossessed
and the homeless on the Underground
angry with complacency
and the pietistic rule of law and order

Angry at jejune Revisionists
as at ill-informed intransigence
at good poetry in bad translation
angry with committee-men
calling in on self-promotion
angry with sleeveens
obsequious and reverential
at funerals the morning after
when embarrassments have been
disposed of decently
and safely laid to rest

Angry with the grunt and
duck-billed platitude
that telegraph the Tory message

and all lick-spittle merchants
touters of received opinions
and received pronunciations
angry at over-simplifiers
canting boors and bully-boys
and anyone who takes
common human courtesy for weakness

And I am angry still
angry with myself
for being there at all
angry with myself for keeping silent
angry with my memories
of taking to the hills
angry with myself
for wasting time in folly
angry with myself in truth —
and this is folly too
angry pointlessly with you
for not being someone else

11.

Where did you go dead fathers
we send out letters no-one answers

Niall son we are I think
                    mad parachutists
dropping through a tiny patch of sky
and landing nowhere —
that's who we are
people of the Ice Queen
the sunset
and the Hag of Beare
that's what we have become

where did you go dead fathers
out past the morning ships
leaving me here on the shore

When I was twelve or so
in Blackrock Baths
a naked man attacked me once
he spat and said — you
you're cultured Irish
you play the harp...

What hidden businesses
were going on there?
What contorted angers
hatred and disgust?

where are you gone dead fathers
who walked on empty Sunday paths

Oh child I wish that I did —
and if only he knew the half of it
where are you now dead fathers
who understood music and numbers

This time last year
standing in the dark in Moscow airport
at the baggage carousel
I met a woman in a stetson
an urgent messenger from home
who said —

    You know? In the madhouse
the general opinion was — and
this they consoled themselves with —
that whatever about the rest

there was one —
there was one who hadn't a hope
in hell
        not a hope in hell
not a hope not one
of coming through —
        and that was you

where did you go dead fathers
who understood poetry — life without hope
or did she think I hadn't noticed?

Son did I tell you
one time I was happiest?
In the Krassikov's orchard
out past Tchekova
digging a hole in the Russian earth

turning over the Russian earth
without thought
        just that
digging a hole for rotten apples
digging a hole among the birches

12.

When will we set out again
to look for Craggaunowen?
Or can such sudden
rightness be repeated?

To be going home like Marco Polo
Coming home like Carolan
That red leaf

on the steps of the big stone House
such a sudden splash
of scarlet —
the outline of a snow-flake
starfish and anchor

The crystals call us back
and the leaves
that fall into our rooms at night

But call us back to what — to sit
at the foot of the stairs
in the hall composing
farewells to music and to poetry

And we come back from wandering
to find ourselves foreign
foreign to the streets of childhood
new buildings fill the gaps
in memory — new voices words and accents
occupy our thoughts

Children grow that much bigger
that much older
in this Republic of the Mind
we carry with us
there is no preventing
new alliances of monsters
the idiot jeers that echo
from the school-yard
or the terrible simpering faces
of people who were young with us

You find that you have
spent your life

fighting with monsters
arguing one agenda
discussing one set of problems
sorting out one situation
until all-and-nothing changes

Not easy to be fluid
as Ivan Malinovski was
as I saw him here
in front of the fire
in Selskar Terrace
untouched and strange
in knee-length britches
speaking Critiques for Himself —
and even if one were
we don't have another lifetime
for a second run at it

Maybe that's why the
Jesuit student of metaphysics
hoping for poetry
made all his notes in prose
a mistake a mistake

With one chance only
to hit the plateau of desire
I can go back in time
and just for now —

Stopped on suspicion
by the police in New Ross
Washed away by the rain
before welcome in West Cork
Best of MacElligott's
welcomes in Kerry

Warmth and shelter in Kilkee
before the sea froze over

Stung by the wind
above Loop Head — now
your grandson sits beside me
as we drive the empty
road for Ennis
drinking Seven Up
eating a pizza —
and what are we doing
but looking
looking for the country
where we are not foreign

rolling in the Van
with the windows open
and together
we're searching for Craggaunowen

FROM JUMPING TO THE LOOP

Today looking over
the ocean to Tarbert

Considering all the way
out to the Loop

How North African dope
floats in on the beaches

Where help never came
from Prince or from Pope

How the Police and the Excise
directing the seizures

Don't leave us a morsel
for symbol or toke –

When the continents drift
what foundation is left

What reality's left
when identities shift

Or what's at the end of
the movement of peoples

But to lie at the edge
of a field in a ditch?

And when my time is come
I won't stick around

On the day I turn sixty
I'll leave for the south

To lean on a wall
at some wide river's mouth

In a westerly wind
in a blizzard of doubt

To keep my own die-hard
appointment with – no

But I swear that
I'll be there and wait

For the end to approach
in stone bed or stone boat

That is all by my oath
but I ask :

Will it make its way in
by the palm of my hand?

Or the hole
in the horn of my foot?

Thinking of May 1994: From Moveen West in the County Clare

1.

All that fortnight I was waking up
to bird-song early in the Post Bellum South –
all night the trains on the Norfolk Southern
cut slow tunnels through the dark
and the sound of swings and children's voices
from Walter Ollte's across the road
came to me cool after breakfast –

The end of April on Walpurgissnacht
I found a place to sit
beneath a Maple and a Tulip tree
all afternoon the heat climbed up
and unfamiliar flowers dropped like fruit
hot strong and sweet as tea at a fair –
confusing geographies and language
in the smell of white-pine boxwood briar
the countryside had caught me on the hop

As in the Ozarks too it caught me
the panoramic lake and trees
called up Italian sounds and voices
archipelagoes of Archimago – the eerie image
of a bathing pool with no one there
and I
not having the questions to put
yet alone being able to interpret answers
as blind as the next at Newgrange

Without the history of townlands
I cannot scan the landscape
and what's left becomes
a series of synapses: of why
I didn't make it to the Jesse James Museum
to read a poem in South Missouri
for Jesse and the boys like Vera Lynn –
too chary maybe of cant or kitsch
of tying yellow ribbons and the rest?
Too superior by half: by half not good enough

The mind picks up on what it can – and I
see Tchekov's workplace here
by the lake at Table Rock
in the little wooden bell-tower
of the sundeck of a herb-farm – and in Virginia
the lines of the Gazebo on the lawn
before the timbered house at Mount San Angelo:
in Tchekova that's also how it is
a yachting superstructure
improbably set inland among trees – a
landlocked photograph:
his postcard –
My home where I Wrote the Seagull

2.

Time and a little space
is all our statutory need – a little
time and warmth and those
appointments that we do not keep
admissions that we do not make to Immigration
the carnage at the river
in the dark parts of the mind

the long compulsion to the cliff path
and in St Isaac's Square St Petersburg
the poet dangling
terror
in the Hotel d'Angleterre

The seabird swims in air
we move in time and memory
with moments shared of history and focus
ambushed by perception:
perhaps a woman laughing in the doorway
of a Moscow block of flats at night
among October trees on Lenin Heights —
at once
significant and meaningless
as sunlit sparks of rain that sting
my window-pane today in Co Clare

For nothing is as is
what's real stays real despite revision —
the human form blends into landscape
and reverse --
a red bird burning in a bush
and how sensuous become the hollows
in the prairie of the belly
the roll of haunches curving into shadow
that fringe of hair beside the lake
the thrust of wind through pinions

as we fly out to sea
at last
carefree above the precipice
the thrust of wind through pinions

NEW POEMS

I gCuimhne Raifteirí: Bherginia

Thank you April thank you
for the photographs
these pictures that you took
and sent me – I look old
as it's true that I am
standing there old on the lawn
near where the tulip trees begin
standing a little apart
and not caught up with clutching
after youth not yet
            and I see that
the broken nose is there
which is also right – despite the Zodiac
and script I've made
old jig-saw bones in the end
survival reassurance
that I'm here
            though true not as fast
on my feet as I was
thirty years ago
in Spain this month – before
spring doors clicked shut
on broken promises and unmade dates
before I learned the truth
when my nose was straight
and my head was bent
to walk bad roads in broken boots

STREET SCENES: THE RANELAGH ROAD

The elderly man who sits
in the sun today
in Manders Terrace
is the same
who called at my door
last year with news of birds

Without preamble:
the swans are dying he said
when I opened the door –
gesturing into the air
the swans are dying
oh God the swans
the swans the swans the swans

Today it's the rats
are the trouble: the rats
hereabouts who live
in the trunk of a hollow tree

The rats and also another
old man
who pushes a bike
up the Ranelagh Road –
and I haven't seen him for weeks
he says not for weeks
have you? Have you seen him
or where could he be?

He's a skilled man too
he says – for he took a plant
one day like that one there
took out the knife

squinted along the length of the stick
sharpened the ends
and fashioned
a handle like you'd get on a hurley

But what would he want
with that? What would
he want that for?

And I don't know he
answers himself –
but a skilled man surely
and I haven't seen him this month or so
though I travel a lot myself
and I see him sometimes
in Sandymount
for that's where he sleeps you
know
in Sandymount there by the sea

And a skilled man surely –
but what would he want
with a stick like that?
With the two ends sharp
like that –
and a handle like
you'd get on a hurley?

FOR PAT KAUFMAN: MAKER

Last night I saw the mist
lit up around the Empire State
and thought of you
finding your sense in shapes
in distance and perspective
in collage
            blue lights
above the street
and images that shift   {
from the familiar to the strange
however many times I look

and this is how it was
a dinner that we ate Eiléan and I
in a restaurant
in Cardinal Lemoine
the death-bed house of Paul Verlaine

Le mystère?
enfin c'est Le Mystère
and then when I ordered it
            the mystery ran out:
plus de mystère
the waiter said
le mystère n'existe plus

in the room beneath the room
where Verlaine died

Last night I saw the mist
around the Empire State lit up
with greens and blues
and shapes

177

from the other side of sleep

and thought of you
at work
and poems yet to make

the mystery still exists I thought
the mystery exists all right

Pensando Leopardi

1.

On the far side of
the mountain
climbing the stony path
I heard your voice
electric
well-remembered
hard-t accent
filling the space at noon
calling me north
to sea and slip
calling me back
to the stony beach

Maga Circe
word and voice: —

This is the fold in time
and here the hole in the rock
let you make life
and music start again
if there be music left
If I have music left

I have come so far
from the sea —
let there be music left

2.

Have I been
misled by the map —

179

my August tracks
are where
at last the world dries up —
I love the light
and dust
the now of things
of heat-cracked earth
loose piebald quills of porcupines
across the path
and down below
the harvest sunflowers
burnt to black

Up here
the macchia remains
my sun-dried
underwater garden —
the mountain too an island
full of voices
until walking over
all these hills
and keeping silence
itself appears invented purpose
that we survive
keep faith —
that there be music left

3.

The orioles return
each year
to light among the figs

...and I
have come so far
from the sea
blue sloes line the ditch
oak apples strew the path
and all I have done
with my summer days
is walk and think and walk —
if nothing
comes of nothing
can nothing come of this
nothing come of nothing
and let there be music left

OCEAN SOLSTICE:

This was this is
remembered time and place
at midnight
and the white lights
of the solstice

Here tonight:
this now – a headland
three sides bordered
by the sea below
where sea-roads fantail
into highways
stretching South and West

And
from the midnight West
of backlit land and sky
reflected sea-light of the ocean
makes it right
to read-off time in snatches

And I can almost clearly see
your own translucent walk
in opaque light outlined among
New Zealand wind-break shrubs
Circe gliding down
the hill-slope to the road
the road beneath

Above the sea beneath the moon
where I am waiting still
time slips

light floats
the sea gives back –
you make no seeming contact
with the earth

And this is music now
remembered
a slow-air of desire –
my mother's song I sang for you
and with the Gaelic this:

this music in my head
Salva me et voca me
Che faro senz' Euridyce?

CIRCE

The shadow
on the lung
I knew
was there reveals
the shadow

The shadow
in the brain
is real
and grows
and daily tells

The shadow
in the heart
is hot and red
is blood
bright blood

The shadow
on the road
is sudden
hard and quick
take care

The shadow
beating
in the thighs
remains always
the shadow

The shadow
waiting in the sky
anneals
restores us
to the sun

1 — CLADNAGEERAGH

Wish the heron well for me
the curlew in the rain
and the kestrel on the wind
wish them well for me do
the gulls at their moorings
sheep in the ring-fort
boats taking shelter
and shrubs of the storm-break

As the moon to the sea
is the hare on the mountain
my heart to him too
small un-named creature –
free to go where the road goes
under the lights of your house

2 — DECEMBER 31ST 1998

For a moderate while there
fifteen years or so
I had a notion
of what was going on —
But now I'm afraid
it's Planet Pluto again
time for me to be moving
further and further out

Back to my lump of dusty ice
beyond the point of vision
in the meantime
I have to keep walking
talking making notes
calibrating the tilt of the telescope

3 — FOR MAIREAD AND PADDY LINEEN AT CHRISTMAS

Blue white and red
are the sheep in the road
at Corrymore —
blue white and red
chrysanthemum sheep
of the Marseilleise
and the French Republic:
tricoloured partisans

And is that not the cup
of the winds up there
where water is moving light
and rustle of grass and scratch
of feather on rocks
carved out by time and ice

TIERRA DEL FUEGO

I walked across to the island
carrying sand and fire —
breathing the sulphur
of dead volcanoes hearing
the morning cock at the cross-roads
echo of gulls on salt-flats
echo of dogs across the ice-floes
dogs with yellow teeth
nothing moved in the ice-world
nobody called in the wind

None from before the guns and plague
people of snow and fire
from before the spillage for gold
before the orders to shoot on sight
before the agent posted the notice
'A Pound for an Indian's Ears
& More Again for a Woman's Breasts'
before words caught in the throat
what birds flew in the hail then
what did we see looking North

Our fires that were not beacons
people of fire we were —
to be discovered and displayed
naked against the light
in the ring in an iron cage
and space alone is left
in middens of food and ash —
only the odd bleak mound
of oyster shells and bones of birds
and ice and wood and rock
what was the sign by your foot
where was the lie of the path

All the howling night these waves
have crashed against the rocks
and rocks against the hills -
you on the bridge to the island walking
you lunar human naked bare
straining to see in the dark
what did the mirror show you
what did you see in the light

STEPHEN'S GREEN: FEBRUARY 1998

Almost fifty years ago
that I sat here a child of six
dealing with the real –
the shadow on my lung
and the keeper with the stick
who ran to put me out

Thirty-five years since
I stood here – my arm
around a fair-haired girl
dealing with the real
and the keeper with the stick
who tried to drive us out

Today I sit here in the sun
dealing with the real
and the keeper with the stick
is nowhere to be seen –
this side of fifty years
he is younger than myself

Than all of my selves
I am older than the rocks
in the rockery-garden
older than the haunted head
of Mangan – older than
the angel waiting at the gate

SOLSTICE

I brushed ashes
on the path today — swept powdered
bone into the cracks

Between
the brown silica bricks
beneath my feet

The city-garden bricks
of childhood
sunlight glinting quartz

Etched pictographs —
a rocky place suspended
in the mind at night

The same as when
apart we watched
the marvellous comet — above

A stony beach
for you - for me the sky at Easter
under Panicale...

At Merrion Gates tonight
I watched the clouds outlined above
the hospital and sea

And further North
the nimbus Arctic-Circle light
affirming absences

And distance —
the empty space between the waves
that carry off the shore

As I brush ash and bone
into the path
push dust into the cracks

Cante Jondo

I made my way to Mexico
through fields of biting rain

I saw a bird with wooden wings
saw sails that turned the wind

If I should wake tomorrow
to find the mountains gone

Could I make my way to Mexico
and the hall of the yellow sun?

The night I slept in Mexico
a blue bird on the wall

An Aztec moon with open eyes
was honey all night long

But morning came with ocean-light
and leached away the road

These nights I look for Mexico
my eyes the colour of blood

In Spello: Scáthach

Tonight
in Spello
before we go on stage
and looking eastward
to the hills
and Col Fiorito
earthquake country
I think of you
Scáthach

Sex and fire —
and how I might
come looking now
to find you
there
among the Sybils
if I'd the strength
to go back
forty years
and find us waiting

Comrade-
lover
from Sebastopol
my vendengeuse
copain
and fellow-traveller
so long ago
...*ou allez-vous comme ça*...
in torn clothes
my old
co-veteran of distance
before the auto-routes

Those two
long since gone to ground
among mimosas

Old doors
have opened up
and closed
in Sainte-Geneviève
the police
have been and gone
the gutters
are clean
and the kerbs straight
and there isn't
a sign of us —
not an empty bottle
or broken boot
in sight

Just a cough
and catch of breath
today
in a room
on the plain below
Assisi:

a middle-aged man
in the afternoon
who clings to sleep
with
the shutters closed

SERIAL

I dreamt of drink again last night
of days in public houses without pause
and finding out the night's companions' names
the morning after in the hours
before the bars had opened up again –
I dreamt of this and spending years
remaining faithful to an act of hope
steering by unauthenticated stars
when others found out where the world begins
where people pay their way
foreclose on debt call in on favours done
die honoured in the end among their own –
I closed my eyes and set my sights upon
damp alleyways of Eden in the dawn

EAST ROAD EAST WALL

There was sunlight in the yard
when I broke my toe
five years of age
fifty years ago
in the hall the Japanese umbrellas
in the parlour
the mandolin and concertina
always sunlight in the yard
and heaps of coal
lights from the locomotives after dark –
I know
the heat from the fire-box glow
in Westerns

In the roof there were pointed windows
behind the house
the verandah
trainlines leading to the docks
down there where my green balloon
sailed off
all those missing years ago

And a journey with my mother
across Dublin
past the Custom House —
oh don't put me
in there — I said
don't ever put me in there —
three of us up
on a donkey and cart
moving my grandfather's piano
me and my mother
and the one-armed driver

my mother engaged —
piano-mover with a heart condition

Anchored in time
and light – a child
in Gandon's open space
where my
one-legged great-grand-uncle
navigated yet another
nautical academy

the first left sailing empty
abandoned in Belfast

Behind us all the afternoon
the East Wall in the sun
the parish register
of Lawrence O Toole's —
recording the marriage of Wooloughan and Dias
and where was she from I wonder
the Iberian name at last
the further I go
the nearer I get
get back
            to that peninsula
travelling South to Pembroke Street

Travelling now to
Clonskeagh
half a century later
across the river and city
across the Grand Canal
(that's my house there
            in Ranelagh

that's where my son lives
          and I
hold onto this
         I think
and that's where I was born
down there
in Upper Leeson Street)

On the anniversary of my father's death
I am looking toward
Clonskeagh
where my mother is slowly dying
and saying her fragments of prayers
from childhood — oh
in this January month
as always
the trees are bare
I see too clear

In the pumping-station
I paused today
there was sunlight
in the yard
the engineer says
there is always sunlight here
he says —
not true I know
but I know what he means
for this was the place for photographs
on kitchen chairs
hauled into daylight
my people sat here
afternoons

This week
they begin to knock the house
that was Billy Woods's home:
and Norah Wooloughan's

the Japanese umbrellas
the mandolin and concertina
the columned clock on the mantel
their three sons

the heaps of coal
the puff and steam of locomotives
and the shaking great pump-engines
gone

outside the bricked-up
parlour window
a palm tree in a pot lives on

January 1999

LOBELIAS: ACHILL ISLAND

(for Donald Sur)

A thousand flowers
lit up
the accidental roads

That brought us here
wherever
here is now –

Cool blue plaster
clusters
round the feet of saints

In empty childhood
country
churches long ago

Or green hydrangeas
in country gardens –
blue copper verdigris:

Korean blue and green
make up
one colour kept for nature

Blue and green
together –
Chung Sun told me this:

And dancing blue lobelias
just now
upon the window-sill

Tip-step me into suddenness
my copper
nerves stripped bare

At sight of sea and land
beyond
the sea and further tumbling sky

Repeated land and sky
and layers
of sea and land and sky again

Unending green all blue
all colours
breath – all movement all

All colours
flow
all colours – all

all movement air
until

all colour
green and blue

Sagra Della Pannocchia

Good Mrs Corncob here we are
at the end of another year
carrying on with what we do
and no nearer to the middle of the earth
thank God – we're human still
distracted daily by our friends

They tell me you've been moved
sideways into Agriculture:
computing the quotas from Brussels
keeping an eye on the countryside –
that dirty dog that posed
without a stitch for P Vannucci

Myself I've been lying low
fading into the land once more
without very much of a stitch
and less in the way of bare ambition
taking walks and making poems
moving in and out of language

Moving in and out of sunlight
up and down the hills – and one
of these days it will do for me
tomorrow or twenty years from now
put a stop to plays on words – my
exhortations in the *orto*

And it doesn't trouble me that
my Uncle Pat fifty years ago
was found alone at the side of the path
to his house: the place was his own

and the time and his age – my pity
for those who live on

The angry differing petulant same
stuck in the family script:
I have the hills to walk it away —
wondering how Maestro Zubitski is
and how I am myself – nothing is true
where there are no gipsies

No divergence and dissent
true for Plato true for Panicale —
true for us and let's agree
we never could be One —
or not so you'd know: our other
us unpurified uncleansed

Rathlin Island: Sept 18th 1999

And Ballycastle – Ita said –
lit up like Monte Carlo

At night across the water
Now all night all day

The wind
has rattled the windows

On energies
inside the house and out

Image seeking image
deep-sea creatures far below

The seal-shapes
bobbing in the harbour

The ferry tied
and jumping at the quay

Rathlin like a
fine-chipped flint

Sits in the ocean
on the head of Ireland

Lights sweeping
over Moyle and North Atlantic

Will there be sunflowers
there I asked

Before I'd been
to the upland lakes

Before I'd seen
the rain-soaked moon

Will there
be sunflowers there

And there were –
in the Manor House

On Church Bay
behind the rattling wind

Behind the
Gages' Georgian Walls

Sunflowers
in the corridors

Sunflowers passed from
hand to hand

The honey-light of
wood

Of tea
in yellow cups

Like butterflies
in summer on a wall

Floating cups
and yellow saucers

Flowers orbiting
the sun —

And Ballycastle
out across the water

Where seven tide-runs
meet

Far away
miraculous

Posting itself
to Comgal's island:

As Ita said
as we walked home

Between the lamps
and dark

And leather boats
of wanderers

Like Samarkand
or Capricorn

Like Monte Carlo
all lit up

NA hEALLAÍ

This is my ship
and the storm outside is you

all of you — and absence
irregular bursts of thunder

again I close the shutters
open them

throw logs on the fire
and wonder at the early dark

Tonight
I must wash the floors

tomorrow strip the bed
turn off the water

in the pipes — pack my bags
and leave again

Five days now I've been
imprisoned

with that ambivalent
pronoun *you* —

that signifies presence
absence silence

do *you* remember
reading to me

for the sick and dying
in the black-bound

Book of
Common Prayer

to comfort me keep me
from drowning

in delirium
being lost in absence

Until now: and the only *you*
I can speak to

is absence is silence
is silence is distance

is absence is distance
is you

WOTAN'S FEAST

(for Donald Sur)

1.
For fourteen days
the rain
had prowled the yards
in Boston

2.
Inside for the feast
there were
letters and words
to stick on the fridge –
family and
a book on Architecture

crispy-chicken
lobster

smoked salmon
cauliflower

beef bean-curds
broccoli

saumon au gratin
roast-duck

oyster-pancakes
prawns

carrots
asparagus cheese

and a birthday cake
like a curling-stone

3.
outside in the rain
the father and son
I've been seeing all day
speaking English Russian
Greek Haitian
Portuguese –
(obrigado I say *obrigado)*

4.
Would it matter in the end
if there were no candles
no candles there
but there were
or even if you were not there
but you were
for Sefauchi's Farewell
played
in the night
before Aughrim

5.
Donald –
in times of rain
and days and nights
of rain-to-come

letters and words
to stick on the fridge
and a birthday cake
like a curling-stone

Street Scenes: Neighbours

The little birds
is cunts
said my neighbour
is cunts
the little birds
and they eat everything

And I see
they're cutting
the trees in Manders
and I hope they do
them fuckers too

Waving his fist
at the stand of trees
down at the bottom
of my garden

But the little birds
is the hoors

Mind you — he
continues
spotting a neighbour
from five doors down —

There's a queer
lot of cunts
that live around here
when you
come to think about it

THE ASPECT OF THE RUSSIAN VERB

(for Giuseppe Santarella)

The aspect of the verb
I go
depends on if I go on foot
or ride
or with another
take a bus
or with such or such an end in view

And if I go from here
to there
(perhaps intending first
to travel somewhere else)
my end may be decided in the end
on pure semantics

Giuseppe tells me
that's why Russians shout
shto shto
what what
when asked directions:
needing you to clarify
the aspects
the semantics of the verb:

Astray
in Longford yesterday
a young man with a shotgun
held the police at bay –
a night and day with
shotgun-blasts and music:

He is very agitated
said the tellymen portentously —
we've heard loud music
he's been playing music loud
all afternoon
the volume turned up full:
they do not say
what music he is playing –
what he hears –
nor care
to clarify the aspects of the verb:

The verbs *to be to die*
to love to hear – last night we heard
the young man
and his music both were gone
shot dead
and silent cold
an end to movement
and to music and to verbs:

The lilac's out today
beneath my window –
Niall plays loud music here
he beats the drums
and plays the music loud
all afternoon –
this place being where he lives

within the aspect of the verb
I hope
the lilac blooms for him

April 21st 2000 Niall's Birthday

IMMAGINE UOMINI: FOR PAUL ON HIS FIFTIETH

It was our Sicilian friend
il barbiere di Magione
who told us of one another:
Lei conosce
il Professore Irlandese
con barba rossa?
E conosce lei
lo scrittore Irlandese
con barba nera?

He too is dead now
gone to rest
and the scaffolding is down
from
the tower of the Longobardi
first time
in twenty years
I've seen it naked
bare-faced stone

The twenty years I've seen
the beard
sea-change
from black to grey
iron
in the colour of the lake
iron in the soul and eyes

Roux et noir
it comes to this –
our personal
acquaintance with mythologies:

across the road
from my new-barbered head
just now —
I'm walking home —
I see the same three aged men
in shade
beside the refuse bins
upon the same three
ancient seats

Beneath the skin
three fates
measuring out the thread
by knots:
for generations
playing cards
discussing time and place